THE HEART OF
VOCAL HARMONY

musicPRO
guides

THE HEART OF
VOCAL HARMONY

Emotional Expression in **GROUP SINGING**

Deke Sharon

Hal Leonard Books
An Imprint of Hal Leonard Corporation

Published in 2016 by Hal Leonard Books
An Imprint of Hal Leonard Corporation
7777 West Bluemound Road
Milwaukee, WI 53213

Trade Book Division Editorial Offices
33 Plymouth St., Montclair, NJ 07042

Printed in the United States of America

Book design by John J. Flannery

Library of Congress Cataloging-in-Publication Data

Names: Sharon, Deke.
Title: The heart of vocal harmony : emotional expression in group singing /Deke Sharon.
Description: Montclair, NJ : Hal Leonard Books, 2016. | Series: Music pro guides | Includes bibliographical references.
Identifiers: LCCN 2016011656 | ISBN 9781495057830 (pbk.)
Subjects: LCSH: Choral singing--Instruction and study. | Emotions in music.
Classification: LCC MT875 .S515 2016 | DDC 782.5/143--dc23
LC record available at http://lccn.loc.gov/2016011656

ISBN: 978-1-4950-5783-0

www.halleonardbooks.com

To sing a wrong note is insignificant.
To sing without passion is inexcusable.
—LUDWIG VAN BEETHOVEN

Contents

CHOICES

MEANINGS

PERSPECTIVES

TECHNIQUES

CONSIDERATIONS

MOTIVATIONS

INSIGHTS

CONTENTS

Aesop's Fable: The Wind and the Sun

The Wind and the Sun were having an argument about which was more powerful when they saw a traveler walking below. They agreed that they could settle their bet by seeing who could make the man remove his coat. The wind went first, blowing as hard as he could, but the more he blew, the more firmly the man wrapped the coat around himself. Then the sun came out from behind a cloud and shone gently, and the man removed the coat.

Dedication

*The young, free to act on their initiative,
can lead their elders in the direction of the unknown.*
—MARGARET MEAD

When it comes to greatness in music, people invariably turn to professionals. However, the greatest lessons I've recently learned in vocal harmony have come at the hands of three amazing groups of high school singers.

The first is Oakland School for the Arts' Vocal Rush, created and directed by contemporary a cappella legend Lisa Forkish (the creator and music director of collegiate a cappella phenomenon U. Oregon Divisi, who were the blueprint for the Barden Bellas in *Pitch Perfect*).

What struck me when working with Vocal Rush was not their technical excellence but their emotional availability. They would deliver a song with a rawness and presence that was unheard of in high school a cappella, which found itself too often obsessed with perfect tuning and trophies from choral festivals. It was as if Vocal Rush had hit the reset button, saying, "Hey! Over here! This is what teenagers should sound like, should look like, should be like while singing!" and the result was and remains a revelation. They have won the International Championship of High School A Cappella (ICHSA) an unprecedented three out of four consecutive years and have made most of what happens in high school auditoriums feel trite. They sing songs with meaning, songs with a message, and they deliver that message with the passion that only a teenager can bring to bear.

The second group is OneVoice from Briarcrest Christian School. This group, under the direction of J.D. Frizzell, has as their mission emotional integrity. To hear them sing, to watch a performance is very different from Vocal Rush and yet no less compelling. If you were to say, "Sure, those Oakland kids at the arts school are future pop stars; what about the rest of us?" Briarcrest is your answer. They strike you as the kind of squeaky clean, suburban college prep kids that would stand on risers and sing beautiful chords with bored, glazed eyes . . . and yet they don't. At the end of a song they have tears welling up in their eyes, and so do you. In the few opportunities I've had to work with them we immediately started at the highest level, discussing a song's message and what these singers could bring to it from their experience and their hearts—staying just barely on the safe side of the most powerful emotions in order to share them unforgettably with an audience.

Finally, my new television family, Stay Tuned from Cherry Hill East in New Jersey, under the direction of Heather Lockart. Together, while surviving the chaos of a new reality show, we shared the responsibility to show the nation for the first time what real high school a cappella could and should be. The group was not a class but rather an after-school activity, and although they were initially unfocused, they are incredible people with big hearts. Making the show was stressful, confusing, and in many ways the exact opposite of the environment you'd think would be conducive to emotional openness (the presence of cameras everywhere has a chilling effect), and yet they were brave, they were persistent, they were real. If Vocal Rush showed that it could be done, and OneVoice showed that you didn't have to be street-wise future pop stars to do it, Stay Tuned showed that it could be done by anyone. They didn't have great voices or a daily music class together. They were diverse, unfocused, exhausted at the end of long school days, at the end of a long school year. And yet they did it: in eight short weeks we created real music together.

We as a society are obsessed with teenage culture and dissect it endlessly through movies, television shows, novels, and the like. And yet, when we do, it's through the filter of rose-colored lenses, with actors far beyond their high school years (look at *Glee*, or the movie *Grease* . . . why are there so many twentysomething and even thirtysomething individuals acting like they're fifteen?). These three groups have given the world insight into modern teenage culture as teenagers. They speak a truth that we're all eager to hear and finally can.

For this reason, I dedicate this book to them, and to all the other high school singers, present, past, and future, who stand on stage and sing something real. Please know that what you do is of immense importance, and through your hard work and honesty we are all learning what it means to be you and how to express that on stage, showing the world the heart of vocal harmony.

Preface

The teapot takes in water and gives out tea.
So the human individual takes in anything you give him
and promptly transforms it; he is ready to give you out again
his own reactions—first, in thought and emotion,
then in voice or action.
—Louis MacNeice

My life's work has been to spread harmony through harmony, which has meant different things over time: directing, composing, arranging, coaching, producing, community organizing . . . whatever it takes. It's all part of a long and fortunate journey in the course of which one important realization has come to inform the work that I do. To explain how I arrived at that realization, it may be helpful to say a word about where that journey began.

Even before I could speak, I used to sing myself to sleep and bounce my head on my pillow in rhythm (it wasn't until decades later that I realized I'm literally hard wired for a cappella headbanging!). When I turned five, my mother enrolled me in the children's choir at the local church, then, as soon as I turned seven, in the San Francisco Boys Chorus. By age nine I was in operas with Pavarotti and the like, missing the first month of fourth grade on a tour of Alaska. Throughout elementary school and high school I was in every chorus, every vocal group, every musical without fail. I decided to attend two universities at the same time: the New England Conservatory of Music, so I could have a true immersive musical experience with great musicians, and Tufts University, so I could work with the Beelzebubs (the school's all-male a cappella group), the Tufts Choir, and the West African Drum Ensemble in the context of a traditional liberal arts college.

I had exemplary teachers who taught me very well, and yet I've come to realize that my education was sorely lacking in the most important element of all: emotion. I do not blame my teachers for this, because no one else I've spoken with from my generation got significantly more insight into this topic than I did. A music education does not (or at least did not) include a component of emotional availability, emotional integrity, emotional range and nuance, and yet that's exactly what we demand from our musicians of all styles. It's as though our music culture is designed to teach the grammar and pronunciation of a language with great care, but not how to say anything.

Imagine sixteen Hamlets all on stage side by side speaking and emoting with clarity in unison, and you have a glimpse of the challenge that faces a cappella and choral directors. In a song there is one sound, one vision, one message; and these sixteen people are all responsible for telling the story, sharing the feeling, moving the audience. Any one of them can potentially undermine the experience.

When workshopping a group, be it in private or during an open masterclass, I start by having them sing a song. As soon as they are finished, my first question invariably is some variation on "What does this song mean? What are you saying by singing it?" It is not meant to be a trick question, and yet rarely am I met with more than blank faces. They've studied the notes, they've drilled the rhythms, they've memorized the lyrics, but they've never talked about what purpose any of these musical components serve. And when performers don't grasp the simple emotion that the music was created to express, neither will the audience. Everyone misses out.

It's time to change that. The first step is simply acknowledging that there is a need to consider emotion in rehearsal and performance. For too long has this topic been overlooked in choral and vocal circles, with the vast majority of resources and pedagogy focused on technique and musical precision . . . yet no one chooses the music they listen to at the end of a long day because of how technically perfect it is. They choose music because of how it makes them feel. If emotion is what draws people to music, then it should be central to the way in which we make music.

My intent with this book is to address the process and experience of eliciting clear, focused emotion repeatedly from a group of singers, first in rehearsal and later in performance. It is intended for groups of all sizes and levels, from small to large, young to old, inexperienced to professional. I present it not as the final word but as an early offering in a field of study that is underrepresented in our vocal music culture. In drawing on a range of disciplines and techniques, my hope is to create a menu from which directors and singers may choose as they refine their own techniques, with the hope of many more ideas and breakthroughs to come as this discipline grows and garners more attention.

Just as there is no perfect music, there is no perfect process. As your singers come and go, so may your rehearsal technique change. I did my best to gather the best practices and provide them for you in these pages, buffet style. Choose those that work for you, and disregard those that aren't effective (although I do recommend you try everything at least once; you may be surprised). Moreover, I don't profess to have all of the answers (who does?), so I enlisted the best and brightest minds and voices in vocal harmony today to provide their own insights in response to my open-ended questions. And as you grow as a singer and/or director you will refine your own processes and expand your toolkit. Feel free to scribble in the margins, share best practices, and further broaden the body of knowledge around unified emotional expression in vocal harmony singing. And please share with me any breakthroughs you have so I can incorporate them in my work and forward on the new discoveries to others.

Note: this book is not filled with pithy lists and easy answers. You likely can't open to a chapter in the middle, get a few pointers, and transform your choir's performance. I wish there were a simple process, but if there were, this book wouldn't be needed. Some of the principles are simple, some of the techniques may be obvious, and any can be used alone, but it is in combination that the process is transformative. Much like a vocal ensemble, when all is said and done, the sum is greater than the individual parts.

Above all, trust your instincts. When you find yourself in uncharted territory, as you likely will when a tenor starts unexpectedly crying or an alto refuses to sing a certain song, listen and take the course of action that makes the most sense. Be honest, be open, be kind. Try to get to the bottom of problems, and every day do your best to inspire your singers to be their best. Forgive your imperfections, laugh a lot, and generally "muck about" (as the British say) until you find your way. That's how all real art is made, even though few people admit it. We prefer the myth of the confident pioneer following a bright star only she can see. Yet it is through experimenting, collaborating, and communicating that we learn to connect honestly with an audience—that we learn to give with intention, care, and focus the very thing people most yearn for and need from music.

Although I don't believe in psychic powers, I offer a premonition: one day you'll be in rehearsal completely confused, emotional, uncertain what to do next. Congratulations! That means you're doing it right. Just as you were nervous and unsure when you first sang in a choir, so may you be nervous and unsure when you begin working with these methods. Continue, forge on, using the song's emotion as your guide, and you'll find you've arrived at a very different and far more musically satisfying destination, one you and your audience will appreciate returning to again and again.

Concepts

BASIC PRINCIPLES

Music is the shorthand of emotion.
—Leo Tolstoy

Before we can begin the process of creating emotionally beautiful, powerful, and honest music, it's important to agree on a few basic principles.

What Is Music?

There are many definitions of music, ranging from the mathematical to the experiential. People perceive music differently, and much has changed about the process, form, and sound over time, but one thing remains constant: music is communication.

We humans are animals and, like crickets, songbirds, and whales, we have an inherent desire to create song. In time, as a civilization we developed musical instruments, techniques, styles, and theory, but at its core music remains the act of humans reaching out to and connecting with each other through sound waves.

Music may have lyrics, but often it does not, and yet it always says something. Music that has nothing to say quickly disappears as the songs that speak to universal truths become timeless.

How Is Music Judged?

Music is personal, and as a result there is no ultimate measure, no single cabal of learned musicians that gets to decide what is great and what is not. If you're asked the question "Who is better, Bach or Mozart?" it's clear that there's no single correct answer, and the reason is that each of them reaches us differently, speaks to different people and different emotions. To decide that one is ultimately superior for all people through all time is to fall into the trap of many an intellectual: hubris. We cannot decide for others what is meaningful to them any more than we can decide that an apple is superior to an orange to their taste buds or to society at large. Music lists abound in our culture, and they can be informative as to one person's perspective, but they carry no ultimate weight.

Taking this one step further, it's important to note that although competitions exist within various genres of music, it is impossible to objectively judge music. Singing is not a competitive sport, and although singing competitions abound around the world, it's essential to remember that the opinions of a few judges are just that: opinions.

Through time people and organizations have tried to codify the rules and practices of music such that it can be better judged, but when we look back at those efforts they show themselves to be the result of well-intentioned ignorance. At one point in Western music the tritone was declared "the devil in music," as if such a thing were even possible. Now we relish that sound so thoroughly that it is at the heart of the single most iconic chord progression in Western music: V7–I.

The highest note is not better, although it may be technically impressive. Neither is the lowest pitch, or the fastest rhythm, or the most precisely tuned chord. As much as people relish the thrill of Olympic events, it's impossible to create a counterpart for music.

If you're not convinced by this line of reasoning, let's try a little thought experiment: at the end of a long day, what music do you choose to listen to? If you stated "the most in-tune music I own" then you are one of a kind. The majority of people choose music that makes them feel a certain way. That feeling is the result of effective communication on the part of the musician.

"Ah," but you say, "I demand technical excellence in my music! I have ears that can hear the slightest defect." To this I offer the following examples: Do you like Motown? If you do, you're tolerating vocal harmonies that are, by today's Auto-Tuned standards, wildly out of tune. Do you like Billie Holliday? Her voice is perpetually in the cracks, and her vocal range is barely greater than an octave. Do you enjoy the voices of Bob Dylan, Randy Newman, Tom Waits? Likely you own some music performed by vocalists who wouldn't even make it onto *American Idol*, let alone win. Even a timeless icon like David Bowie, a pioneer in popular music who constantly reinvented himself, would not land a gig as a session singer.

Still not convinced? Let's consider cool jazz, a style of music that is so very technically demanding and complex that, true to its name, it leaves some people feeling cold. Surely the most demanding musical perfectionist can find repose in these cerebral sounds? Let's look at the single best-selling jazz album of all time, Miles Davis's *Kind of Blue*. It's imperfect. Gloriously, obviously imperfect. You can hear Miles play pitches that are out of tune, even play squelchy notes that a music teacher would criticize for their technical sloppiness. Has that eroded the album's efficacy? No; in fact, I think it has improved it, making it more accessible to the untrained ear. It's music that is played by legends with technical excellence and yet also reflects a measure of abandon, not falling into the trap of perfection over mood and emotion.

The Message

This is my ultimate point: your goal as a singer, as a director, as a musician is to recognize that emotion in a musical performance is more important than perfection. Hone your craft, tune your choir, exercise your voice so you can sing gloriously high notes and hold a pitch for an impossibly long time, but never think that this is the point of music. This is elocution, not meaning. The world would rather hear a passionate speech delivered with a couple of imperfections than a perfectly pronounced speech that's without heart.

Am I setting up a false dichotomy? Isn't it possible to have both technical excellence and emotional content in a musical performance? Absolutely. But at some point you will have to make a choice: what is more important? How are you spending your limited rehearsal time? What are you doing on stage? What does your audience want from you?

They want to feel something and will accept technical imperfection if it's in the service of your message. A cracked note because you choke up while singing a heartfelt passage? Forgivable. But to sing a song without emotion, without meaning? That's not music; that's just organized sound, and as perfect as it is, your listeners will quickly turn to something else that fills their hearts.

The Medium

There is something special and uniquely powerful about vocal harmony.

Before recorded history, before the creation of instruments, there was only the human voice. Throughout history, vocal harmony and a cappella have been central to the development of many styles of music. A study of most aboriginal music, regardless of the region, will find music centering on people singing together.

The term "a cappella" literally means "in the chapel style,"[1] and a cappella music is woven through Western culture, from Gregorian chant (for which our current five-line staff and music notation was created) to madrigals, sea shanties, field hollers, Christmas carols, barbershop, doo-wop, and the current surge of interest in what we call "contemporary a cappella."

In addition, there is something spiritual about the sound of voices together. Some religious denominations emphasize the voice and harmony singing even to the extent of outlawing instruments in their place of worship. Although much of the current popularity of a cappella and harmony singing is thanks to television, movies, and YouTube, the fact remains that this music is most powerful when experienced live, when a group of singers connects to the audience with no effects, no instruments, no video screens or flame pots. There is something supremely affecting about the experience of hearing people creating something beautiful together with only their voices, communicating thoughts and feelings through vocal harmony.

Electric guitars can create a powerful sound, and a symphony orchestra can fill a hall with glorious, resonant music, but when it comes to the conveyance of emotion, there is nothing more immediate and affecting than the human voice and face. From their earliest days, babies mimic their caretakers' faces and voices, and as we grow older we continue to develop and cultivate this essential skill that has allowed humans to work together as we evolved.

The scientific term is "physiological synchrony," and it occurs when we see others expressing emotion in person or on a screen. This effect is so strong that you don't need to know the person or the situation. You can turn on the television and see someone crying, and you're physiologically drawn into that emotion.

To watch a choir expressing with honesty is to watch a dozen, perhaps a hundred faces speaking together through song. This experience is aesthetically very pleasing and physiologically very powerful. A hundred instruments might be able to make a louder sound than a hundred singers, but the singers have the edge when it comes to emotion, especially when they are emoting as a unit.

---

1   Chapels used for small services or events, such as baptisms, at cathedrals and cloisters often lack space for an organ or other instruments, so traditionally the music in these spaces was provided by a group of singers. The term "a cappella" stuck, regardless of location or circumstance, and came to embrace a wide variety of musical styles.

SAY SOMETHING

*We all know that being able to express deep emotion
can literally save a person's life, and suppressing emotion
can kill you both spiritually and physically.*
—LISA KLEYPAS

If you agree that music is a form of communication, then it follows that the most fundamental task you have as a musician, as a singer, is to say something.

If music is a language both embracing and superseding linguistics, a language that is universal and yet very personal, timeless and timely, what exactly does it mean to say something through music? It means that you can say pretty much anything, so long as it is meaningful to you. You can sing about what it felt like to be relegated to the children's table at Thanksgiving when you wanted to sit with the adults, and you can sing about the deep connection you feel when you stare at the stars on a moonless night. If it's poignant to you, then it's potentially poignant to someone else.

If you're singing music casually, for fun, for friends, then there is no reason you should sing anything other than what you want to sing. If you're a professional, with rare exception you shouldn't try to sing something that you don't believe, that you're not feeling, that you can't infuse with your own experience. It would be the same as a public speaker delivering a speech that she doesn't believe. Unless you and all of your singing cohorts are superlative actors, the audience likely will not stay long or remember much. There is too much music, too much media in our world, and if you don't grab someone and hold them, they will change the channel, click away to another video or song, likely never to return.

Therefore, if you want people to hear you, if you want to increase your audience, if you want to touch people, if you want to change lives, if you want music to be your career, your vocation, the task is clear: say something powerful, something meaningful, something that speaks truth. Something that touches people. Something that people will return to and share with friends.

This has never been more important than now, as the world turns its attention to vocal harmony in a way that is utterly unprecedented. My experiences with mass-media vocal harmony began on *The Sing-Off* on NBC, where it was my role to oversee all of the performances. There, I quickly realized that each group's competition wasn't the other groups; it was 199 other channels of television plus everything on the Internet. I had to ensure that each performance by each group was so powerful and compelling that people wouldn't wonder what was on the other channels.

It became clear, immediately, that we needed each group to find the truth in a song right away, and that no group could afford to sing music that wasn't true for them. A nineteen-year-old can't deliver "Still Crazy After All These Years" with anything approaching believability. Perhaps if the song is reworked and there's a level of irony or a greater meaning it might be possible (never say never), but that's a high bar to clear, and most singers, especially amateur singers, are wise to stick to their lives, their experiences, their feelings, their reality.

Why? Because when you're performing, you're creating music for others. It's a gift, and that gift is rarely delivered under ideal circumstances. Perhaps you were first captivated by a particular song late at night, when the mood was just right and the music moved you to want to sing the song yourself. Later you will find yourself onstage needing to recreate that feeling in order for the music to have a message, to have validity. Did you choose a song that you have difficulty feeling, an emotion that eludes you when the circumstances change? Then you chose the wrong song.

Too often groups don't consider this when choosing repertoire. "I like this song" is not the same as "People will want to hear me sing this song because I can make it my own" or even "Lots of people will be drawn to hear me sing this song, despite the countless other versions available to everyone everywhere."

This last point is important to remember: If you're going to sing "When I Was Your Man," by Bruno Mars, you first need to realize that there are probably around 1,000 different versions strewn across the Internet.

Twenty years ago, everyone was happy to hear your a cappella group sing "The Lion Sleeps Tonight," because it was likely the only version they'd hear an a cappella group sing all year. Now everyone has several versions at their fingertips, all day, every day—and they know it. To make your version stand out, to make your performance compelling, you have to be different. You have to be better. And to be better, you have to be honest.

Never before has it mattered so very much that music have a unique, powerful, transcendent quality driven by emotional integrity. Looking at it from the perspective of economic theory, supply is sky-high and rising daily, so as a result demand is at an all-time low.

Yet there is always demand for powerful, awe-inspiring music, there is always demand for something new, and many people are just now discovering the power in an a cappella performance. The purity of unified expression unmediated by machines and technology—just voices and faces, harmonies and emotions—creates an impact that is simply unforgettable.

With apologies to the movie *Field of Dreams*, if you sing something honest and real and meaningful, they will come. Not always, not right away, but in time you will build an audience of people who are eager to hear your next creation because they know that no matter what you deliver, you're delivering something real. You're saying something.

SINGULARITY

We are only as strong as we are united, as weak as we are divided.
—J. K. Rowling

There is nothing more compelling than another person.

We spend our lives interacting with others, watching others, learning from others. With rare exception, the focus of almost every movie, book, story, and song is, in short, another person. We endlessly watch other faces, listen to other voices.

The human voice was the first instrument and remains the most powerful and effective method of musical creation and emotional transference. Certainly other instruments may exceed the human voice in range, but none can make you laugh or cry with the same immediacy.

Whether it be a military display or a marching band, the synchronicity of a group of people is also compelling, but for a different reason. We're awed by the precision of people moving and acting in concert. We are transfixed by the stories and emotions of others, we love the sound of the voice, and we're compelled when we see people acting as one. Put them all together and you have vocal harmony; you have a cappella.

But for these elements to work together with maximum impact, every person needs to be expressing the same emotion at the same time.

An emotional singularity like this doesn't exist elsewhere. People marching in unison need only get their bodies synchronized. When actors share a scene together, each character has his or her own reaction and path, which generally differs from the others'. Moreover, the power of vocal music comes not from singers acting but rather from their honest expression of themselves as themselves.

Herein lies perhaps the biggest challenge facing a choral director: how do you get all of your singers to feel and express in synchronicity while maintaining musical excellence? Unfortunately, the topic of emotional singularity is rarely addressed in rehearsals, in music rooms, in education. It is largely assumed that the people singing Beethoven's Ninth will feel joy when they sing about joy. The music is joyful, the lyrics are joyful, and you might occasionally have the director shout "More joyful!" but that doesn't usually work any more than it works when a loved one tells you "stop feeling so _____ (insert any emotion)."

Perhaps a particular group wouldn't have difficulty expressing the joy of singing while onstage at the end of Beethoven's Ninth (it isn't hard to get swept up into the moment), but what about a wide-ranging concert program in which your group sings a dozen songs, one after another, each with a very different emotional story and journey, and no orchestra on stage playing one of classical music's most iconic celebrations? A solo singer-songwriter is more often than not well versed at moving from one story to the next, but rarely are group harmony singers so deft. The result is a performance in which the efficacy of each song varies greatly, as your singers try to conjure moments as powerful as your best rehearsal, in rapid succession. It's a near impossible task when left to chance and circumstance.

Every group is different, every song is different, every situation is different, and yet we can draw upon a variety of principles drawn from a range of disciplines to help create a consistent emotional performance in your group, song after song.

Preparations

SETTING THE STAGE

When dealing with people, remember you are not dealing with creatures of logic, but creatures of emotion.
—Dale Carnegie

Like plants, emotions can't grow just anywhere. More specifically, people do not feel comfortable and safe digging deep and sharing a range of emotions in all situations and circumstances. For this reason, you need to create a safe environment for your singers to allow for all, even the most sensitive and introverted.

It may seem obvious, but it bears mentioning: your rehearsal location needs to be a safe place for emotional exploration. Are you rehearsing in a chapel with people wandering in and out, or a living room where your roommates are doing the dishes within earshot? You need a place that's yours, where your singers know that the only people who will hear their singing and conversations are those within the group's circle of trust.

Obviously, not every conversation or emotion will be challenging, but when they are you want to be sure everyone feels as though they're among friends. If you're in a classroom or theater you might make a gesture of locking the door(s) so no one can come barging in. If you're rehearsing in your house and you know you'll be dealing with a difficult topic, have your housemates go see a movie that night.

HARMONY THROUGH HARMONY

He who lives in harmony with himself
lives in harmony with the universe.
—MARCUS AURELIUS

You can't create great vocal harmony without interpersonal harmony.

The word harmony has many meanings, and all intersect when a group sings a chord. This may sound like an ephemeral, New Age philosophy, but it's grounded in the most fundamental elements of vocal harmony technique.

If your members aren't getting along, they aren't looking at each other, they aren't listening to each other, they aren't connecting with each other and/or the director. This means they're not paying attention to how their vowels align by observing each other's mouths, they're not listening to differences in pitch and phrasing, and they're not sympathetically breathing as a unit.

When a group smiles together, their tone brightens together and the sound lifts as a unit. If a group is not interacting well, it's very likely that not all of the smiles are genuine, and the effect is not the same. Moreover, the audience can read insincerity, even if only subliminally. We know from experience that people smile with their eyes, and from years of being around children and poorly trained actors we can tell if someone is faking their sadness.

It has been said that some of the actors in our favorite movies did not get along well while shooting the scenes, and yet we can't tell. However, they're professional actors, the best of the best. Your singers are not.

This is a central tenet of the book, so I want to make sure it's clear: actors learn how to create a character and inhabit that character with real emotions. This practice takes years and not everyone is able to do it particularly well, which is why there are not many highly acclaimed actors. Later in this book I will provide techniques drawn from the best practices used by actors, but you cannot expect every person in your group to act his or her way through every moment on stage. Clumsy, artificial moments will undermine the power of sincere emotional conveyance in vocal music. Your singers will have enough of an emotional journey without having to add the weight of hiding negative emotions towards the person standing next to them.

This is not about acting. Your singers need to genuinely connect with the music and genuinely feel. It is not enough for your director to simply say, "Now be angry" or "Sing more joyfully." The problem is not necessarily ignorance on the part of a vocal group as to the meaning of the lyrics or the emotional focus of a song, but rather an inability to shift from the mood they happen to be feeling to the one intended by the composer. Just as in everyday life, one cannot simply hear the words "Be happy!" and immediately feel joy. We cannot play emotions the way we play notes on the keyboard.

Yet vocal harmony is sometimes perfect, with the entire group singing and feeling as a unit. The problem lies in the "sometimes." Sometimes an entire group just happens to be in a particular mood. Sometimes the joy of the last movement of Beethoven's Ninth Symphony truly compels the singers to feel joy even if they're having a bad day. Serendipity happens, but you can't count on it. A methodology and series of techniques are needed for a group to consistently approach a song emotionally.

The members of your group never need be anyone other than themselves, and the techniques offered are all presented from this foundation. We have a wide range of experiences in our lives to draw upon, and whereas we may not have experienced the exact circumstances that unfold in the lyrics of a song, we know the fundamental emotions that they bring forth: anger, joy, fear, and so forth. The process of understanding and drawing forth emotion—your own personal emotion—is at the core of this process and requires a very carefully established environment.

Vocal harmony requires a harmonious environment. What does this mean?

First of all, be it a large or small harmony group, nothing exists beyond or outside of the voices, save for a rehearsal piano or other instrument(s). There is no machinery, no physical infrastructure necessary—only people. As such, the relationships of the people in the group are central to the group's existence, image, and effectiveness.

The question in your mind right now may be "How does my group measure against others when it comes to interpersonal harmony?" To answer that, you might ask:

- Do members of the group frequently chat about each other during rehearsal?
- Is joking within the group (both outwardly spoken and whispered) warmhearted, or does it feel mean-spirited?
- Do the singers trust the director's choices, even when those choices are unusual or unexpected?
- Are singers excited to come to rehearsal and other group events?
- Does the director frequently lose his or her temper? Do singers?
- Do members of the group feel comfortable expressing opinions, even if those opinions or the emotions behind them are difficult?

Whereas there is certainly no single correct way to direct a group or run a rehearsal, there are some common principles that are found in effective, supportive groups:

- There is mutual respect between the director and members.
- Members can disagree and not hold grudges.
- Whereas there may be occasional side-comments or jokes, people remain focused and don't require a great deal of corralling or shushing.
- Members are willing to point out their own mistakes and don't feel judged when they are told they've made a mistake or when they ask for help.
- Members are willing and able to bring up difficult or unpopular opinions, including disagreement with the director (at appropriate times).
- The director and singers approach music with passion, yet never direct negative emotions toward other singers. They realize if there's a conflict, problem, or disagreement that they need to work together to find a common solution.

Mutual admiration, respect, and perhaps even love is at the heart of a great singing group, be it large or small. This is not to say that every group must be without any interpersonal challenges, but rather that the overall character of the group dynamic is a positive, supportive one. Without this atmosphere, emotionally connected singing will be very difficult if not impossible, as several of your members will have their guards up, worried about how they're perceived.

Whatever the specific interpersonal hurdles are within your group, they will almost certainly have to be addressed before or during the processes in this book. Sometimes a director needs to be less of a stern dictator, sometimes a faction of a group needs to be less judgmental, sometimes past grievances must be aired so the people involved can move on. Every group is different, with its own dynamics and history, but one constant holds true regardless of age or circumstance: if you want to create great harmony, your group needs to be harmonious.

DIRECTOR

A director must be a policeman, a midwife, a psychoanalyst,
a sycophant, and a bastard.
—BILLY WILDER

B e it a small vocal band or a choir of 200, almost every group
needs someone to make decisions and act as the focal point
during rehearsals: to lead warm-ups, decide what songs you'll be
rehearsing, and determine when to stop and focus on details. Only
the smallest and most democratic of groups can make do without a
director, and even they will struggle at times when a disagreement
grinds progress to a halt until they can democratically decide what
to do about measure seventeen or if they should eliminate the
second repeat. To make rehearsals the most productive time possible, someone needs to lead.

That someone, often called the music director, is not just a
musician. That person is a leader in many other ways: logistical,
temporal, spiritual, and emotional. To simply choose the person
who knows the most about music to lead your music group is akin
to choosing an engineer to fly your plane. The skills needed to
properly pilot a vocal group include the technical aspects of music,
but reach far beyond them.

What characteristics make for a good director? You want to
evoke

- Respect (without it, each musical direction will be second-
  guessed and often grumbled about)
- Affinity (a coach who is disliked is only able to push the group
  so far)
- Responsiveness (comments should be acted on quickly)
- Openness (members feel comfortable sharing their reactions
  and feelings)
- Attention (a group that is easily distracted or chatters frequently is far less time-effective)

This requires a measure of:

- Charisma (that ineffable quality that makes others want to listen and follow)
- Positivity (negative energy or comments will slow progress and eventually lead to attrition)
- Self-control (one cannot express every feeling and distraction. Directing requires staying on topic and mitigating frustration, anger, and other negative feelings on all but rare occasions)
- Empathy (caring about the individuals in the group will be rewarded by greater openness and commitment)
- Self-effacing sense of humor (directors make mistakes and must be able to laugh at themselves)
- Calm (anxiety is contagious, and is rarely appropriate or effective)

Obviously all directors are human and by definition imperfect. Singers expect this, and a director's flaws, if not overwhelming, can be endearing. No one should expect a director to be above reproach or beyond foibles. The lists above are a measure of important traits and perhaps a list of attributes to be hoped for and worked toward, but by no means should every group expect a perfect director.

In the past, people perhaps looked to and expected a starkly authoritarian leader along the lines of the canonical symphonic director, but this is not the cultural standard in the 21st century, and vocal harmony groups are not full-time professional symphony orchestras headed by demanding, capricious geniuses. What is required of a singer is different from what is required of a flautist or percussionist—though some choirs unfortunately do perform with the lack of facial expression common to most orchestras. A vocal harmony group does not thrive by shutting up and doing exactly as the director says with no input into the music and the process. A bassoonist may be able to play beautifully without liking or feeling any emotion toward the director or the piece of music—and our experience of listening to a bassoon usually doesn't involve staring directly into the instrumentalist's eyes during the performance. But as vocalists, our bodies are our instruments, and audiences are well versed at discerning emotion from the sound of the voice, the way we breathe, and the look on our face. If we don't feel open to the director, or don't feel that the director is open to us, that will be all too clear in our performance.

Nevertheless, a choral director is vested with a certain authority. A rehearsal requires quiet and focus, and the larger the singing group, the less distraction and whispering can be tolerated without creating chaos. This is the challenge facing a choral conductor: running an efficient rehearsal without being a tyrant, keeping people focused without yelling, accepting comments from singers without turning the entire rehearsal into a giant group discussion. Every element of a rehearsal exists on a continuum, and it requires a sensitivity to the group dynamic as well as a sense of priorities (e.g., how much music needs to be learned on a given day) for a great director to know when to stop and when to move on, when to talk and when to sing, when to listen and when to assert her authority.

If this is all confusing, allow the following analogy: the speed at which someone should drive is never constant. It depends on the time of day, the weather, the condition of the roads, the number of turns, the proximity of other cars, and the presence of any emergency. The more you drive, the better you know your car and your roads. The same principles apply to a music director. There are general guidelines (e.g., having your music ready for the concert) and various obstacles (singers who are sick, tardiness, difficult musical passages, emotions, etc.). One's instincts and experience are the best road map of all.

INTRAGROUP RELATIONSHIPS

Nothing truly valuable can be achieved except by the unselfish cooperation of many individuals.
—ALBERT EINSTEIN

First and foremost, the singers in a group need to have a mutual respect for each other. This respect grows over time, supported by four key elements:

1. Talent
2. Enjoyment
3. Timeliness
4. Performances

1. Talent

The overall talent level needs to be within a reasonable range such that no one is holding everyone else back, and no one is so far ahead as to be bored. Obviously, measures can be taken to mitigate broad discrepancies, by giving extra help to the slowest members (additional rehearsal time, learning recordings) and extra responsibility to the superstars (soloist or section leader status, opportunities to direct or arrange a song). The larger the group, the more these issues smooth themselves out, which means small groups will feel more tension between members with vast differences in talent and experience. Having a member in a vocal band far behind the others will quickly present itself as a source of ongoing tension.

2. Enjoyment

If people are having fun together, they will develop positive images of one another. It's not at all necessary for everyone to share the same background, beliefs, or affinities. In fact, one of the greatest benefits of choral singing is its ability to bring together and create friendships between very different members in a community. Those bonds, forged in a positive group atmosphere, will bear dividends in many ways during practice and on stage. Even if they spend little or no time together outside of the practice room, singers who enjoy rehearsing and performing with one another will become friendly and carry positive memories into the future.

3. Timeliness

No one likes to be kept waiting for another member, and the smaller the group, the more essential every voice is to an effective rehearsal or performance. Leaders need to have an efficient method for dealing with problematically tardy members, lest their actions erode others' morale and commitment to timeliness. Starting every rehearsal right on time, even if not all members are present, can be an effective way to drive home the message that one is late.

4. Performances

There comes a time when no more can be taught in rehearsal, and the lessons that need to be learned—both generally (e.g., how to consistently express emotion on stage) and specifically (how a certain arrangement might be improved to heighten its emotional impact)—require an audience. Performing not only brings a group closer with itself and its audiences, it gives rehearsal a purpose and a goal. The more you perform, the easier it will be to motivate singers to memorize their music, remain focused in rehearsal, and realize the importance of infusing each song with emotion.

Unlike a sports team, if you do it right, you "win" every concert you perform. The experience of singing for an audience, the applause and accolades, the increased exposure all create very positive feelings that help a group bond. Creating great music together allows past transgressions and disagreements to be washed away, and with each success your singers will be inspired to double down, to dig more deeply into more complex music and soar together to new heights.

SAFETY

Out of this nettle, danger, we pluck this flower, safety.
—WILLIAM SHAKESPEARE

We're all familiar with the concept of "fight or flight," which is one's animal-instinct-driven reaction to stress. Let's add to that the concept of "freeze," which, like a deer in headlights, is another common reaction.

The "three F's"—fight, flight or freeze—are all an indication of an unsafe emotional environment. If your singers are getting angry (be it about logistics, repertoire, or other members), if you find your membership dwindling because people aren't having a positive experience in the group, or if your performers are freezing up on stage, fearful that they'll be berated for singing a wrong note, the environment needs to be improved before good emotional singing can take place.

Yes, stress can be channeled into music, and it's not uncommon to hear the expression "put it in the music" when something negative happens and feelings are on the brink of overflowing. However this is only possible if your group is unified and supportive. Tragedy happens, both to individual members of a group and to an entire community, and nothing is more healing than vocal music, both to the performers and the audience. A sense of safety is the result of a strong group bond and cannot be expected to come from a group that is feeling threatened or unsupported internally.

OPENNESS

There's just some magic in truth and honesty and openness.
—Frank Ocean

Central to one's ability to be an effective, emotive performer is the concept of openness. All of the members of an ensemble need to feel comfortable being open with their feelings, and the best way to approach this is to discuss the topic at your first rehearsal.

You should outline the following principles:

- Music is communication, not just a collection of notes.
- True, honest music is grounded in real emotion.
- The emotion in the music doesn't "just happen" consistently; it's generated by focused singing.
- For this to happen, singers need an environment free of teasing, ridicule, or judgmental behavior.
- As you discuss emotion in your group, some uncomfortable moments may occur, but this is part of finding the truth in the music.
- The end result of addressing emotion is not only more powerful performances but also more technically proficient ones, because emotion also directly focuses technique (vowel sounds, dynamics, etc.).

It's the rare singer who will not understand and agree to this logic. If you're dealing with young singers who are not entirely comfortable with their emotions, you might approach the discussion a bit differently, bringing up the points one by one rather than in rapid succession, so they have time to fully digest and process each essential step. Additionally, when working with young singers you should choose songs that reflect emotions that are readily accessible and comfortable. Joy is an emotion that no one should be afraid to express, and since singing is such an enjoyable experience it's an excellent first step for everyone (more on this topic later, in the chapter on Joy).

Your best approach in discussing these principles may vary based on the group's interests. For instance, if many of your singers are athletic and responsive to sports analogies, you can use the expressions "going for it with everything you have" and "100 percent dedication and commitment to the song and lyric." In addition, you can explain that, while sports are in the realm of the physical, mental, and emotional elements are still central to success. Similarly, music is a pursuit that blends the physical, mental, and emotional, and precise teamwork is necessary to create great harmony with the other members of your group. On the other hand, if you're in a group that's less competitive and more nurturing, use nurturing analogies. Know your audience and approach this discussion carefully, as it's essential that your singers understand and support this philosophy so that they can fully participate in the next steps.

Avoiding negative, judgmental behavior extends beyond the members of your group. To harshly judge other groups similar to your own is to immediately put some of your singers on the defensive, as they may empathize or see themselves in other performers and performances. You can be clear, honest, and direct in your assessments, but as soon as you cross the line into harshness and a parochial support of your own team over others simply because they're yours, you're forcing your singers into cognitive dissonance.

We are all imperfect, we all have our moments, and it doesn't take much to make some people close down and shut off when they are surrounded by negativity. The Simon Cowells of this world may make for sensational reality television sound bites, but they're toxic to an atmosphere of openness in a vocal harmony group.

BRAVERY

Can a man still be brave if he's afraid?
That is the only time a man can be brave.
—George R. R. Martin

Another essential concept in your group's journey toward collective emotion is that of bravery. People equate bravery with physical deeds, battles against great odds, and personal sacrifice, but increasingly our culture is producing books and movies that reflect bravery in its less violent and more intimate forms, such as telling a friend something difficult or speaking truth to power.

True emotional honesty in front of other people requires bravery. Many would prefer to avoid any public display of intimate feelings, yet it is essential to great musicianship, and it is the reason we're drawn to the greatest performers of all time. Emotional expression is especially difficult when your group is first exploring emotions together. You likely will have a room full of apprehensive singers, and yet someone needs to be the first, and those first singers to take the risk and open up are exhibiting bravery.

Many groups, especially large ones, suffer from herd mentality. People don't want to move away from the pack, be it ahead or behind. In addition, some cultures exhibit "tall poppy syndrome," in which people ridicule successful entrepreneurs and otherwise daring people simply because they have shown themselves to be exceptional (the tall poppies are cut down). This is not as common in America as it is elsewhere, but it's also not unheard of. The combined result of these social forces is that it can be difficult to find someone to take the first step down a new path.

Therefore, when you reframe the process of open emotionality as one of bravery, you're appealing to an important aspect of the human psyche. You're reframing the lone scout as the valiant vanguard, the first into the new land—and, once enough brave souls cross the border and show everyone it's safe, the herd will follow.

SIZE AND SCOPE

It's not the size of the dog in the fight,
it's the size of the fight in the dog.
—Mark Twain

The number of different vocal harmony groups in the world is staggering, ranging from trios to choirs of over 300 in a wide variety of configurations and styles. Although all groups have their own unique elements and challenges, in many ways, the size of a group determines the dynamics of rehearsal and performance, as well as the nature of a director's role. For the purposes of clarity, here is a breakdown of the three major categories of vocal harmony groups:

Band

Although this word originally meant a collective of instrumentalists, "vocal band" or just "band" is a frequent moniker for contemporary a cappella ensembles of three to seven members who each sing their own vocal line at least most of the time ("one on a part"). These ensembles don't follow a conductor on stage and are self-directed in rehearsal, usually relying on a greater measure of democracy and collective input when making decisions both musical and logistical. If one member oversees the musical elements of the group and runs rehearsal, that member is still a fellow singer and also subject to critique from the other members.

Ensemble

A group ranging in size from 8 to 20 members has elements of both a band and a choir. These mid-sized groups sometimes have an external director (especially in the case of a professional group like Chanticleer) but more often this person sings as well and is chosen from within the ranks. Almost all collegiate a cappella groups fall in this range, and with good reason: there are enough members that the group can have a couple of absences without being unable to perform, and yet not so many members as to require risers and a conductor. A common occurrence in these groups is peer leadership, which creates an interesting and sometimes challenging dynamic: as a fellow student, such a leader must decide when to be a leader and when to be a friend, when to be one of the singers and when to direct.

Chorus/Choir

An ensemble of over 20 members almost always has a clearly designated conducting director. Conducting is often a necessity to keep dozens or hundreds of singers together, temporally as well as emotionally. The singers can be elementary school students or senior citizens, but the director is pretty much invariably an adult, and stands apart from the group as the conductor in rehearsal and in performance. Group members' opinions are less often heard for the reason that there are so many people in the room, necessitating that a director wield more power and bear a greater responsibility for the group dynamic.

Fostering Intimacy

When I use the term "group" I am referring to any and all of the above: an ensemble of any size or configuration. The lines between the three configurations blur, such as the rare vocal band that has 9 members, or the select high school chamber choir with 16 members and a faculty director/conductor. As with everything else in this book, apply these techniques as you see fit, modifying them as needed to suit your group's size, technique, and style.

Despite the many commonalities between all vocal harmony groups, there is one important, pronounced difference between large and small groups: intimacy. Every person in a quintet knows the other members very well, whereas the singers in a 200-member chorus might not know the names of half of the other people on stage at any given time. Intimacy and interpersonal connection are central to vocal harmony, so they should be fostered in larger groups. Why? Because small groupings of people

- Allow more introverted members an opportunity to open up and express themselves to others.
- Give everyone more of an opportunity to speak and have his or her voice heard, especially in very large choirs.
- Create less risky opportunities for new ideas to be vetted. Sometimes the craziest ideas are the best, but if the only forum for discussion is in front of the entire choir, they may never be heard.

- Develop expressive confidence. Younger members, quieter members, and newer members alike have a chance to be the focus, which helps reinforce full engagement in group performance.
- Create many new bonds between members that help strengthen everyone's connection to the larger group.
- Facilitate more meaningful "deep" learning, as has been shown in numerous studies. Simply listening to a lecturer is never as effective as having an opportunity to discuss and process new concepts with others.

How does one create opportunities for smaller groupings of members?

- Sectional rehearsals: If your choir isn't too big, or if you have an ensemble, dividing your singers by voice part immediately creates small groups. Regardless of size, you're reducing the number of singers to 25 percent or less, which changes the dynamic.
- Various committees: to decide upon a new logo, design your web site, promote upcoming concerts, choose new repertoire, or any of a hundred other things.
- Performing opportunities for small groups: Your choir may be 200 strong, but if you're going to be delivering singing valentines and the arrangements are only four parts, you can unleash 50 quartets upon your community.

It bears mentioning that the techniques in this book work for all vocal harmony groups. It doesn't matter whether your group is a cappella or performs with piano, guitar, or symphony orchestra. Emotion is emotion; harmony is harmony. In fact, many groups perform both with and without instruments. There is a tendency when performing with instruments for singers to feel less exposed, even able to "hide" behind the instruments. There's also a chance if performing with a large group of instruments that the singers will be influenced by expressionless instrumentalists, or feel as though they can't be seen as well because they're behind the symphony orchestra; or they may be lulled into a trance during long passages during which they have nothing to sing. None of these excuse a performer from powerful emotional singing. Discuss these tendencies and prepare for them so as not to reinforce bad habits and backslide into bored, expressionless singing.

BREAKING DOWN BARRIERS

There are no constraints on the human mind,
no walls around the human spirit, no barriers to our progress
except those we ourselves erect.
—RONALD REAGAN

To access emotion, we must break down the barriers that we have built up over the course of our lives. The end result is a state of being that allows you access to your emotions without having them overwhelm you throughout your day. Great singing doesn't require that you be perpetually emotional, but rather that you create an ongoing openness toward your emotions.

Emotional openness is a state of mind, a willingness, a flexibility, and a freedom to allow oneself to feel emotion. Although this state is easier for some than for others, it's available to all. When we were children, we expressed our emotions very openly. If we didn't, our parents and caregivers would not have known our needs so that they could properly care for us. As we grow older and begin to care for ourselves, we become socialized and learn that expressing our every feeling is not always appropriate, and is sometimes problematic. We are taught by society to hide our feelings at moments when they are not appropriate and over time, we experience less of a connection to the feelings that we suppress.

Openness does not demand that one revert back to the emotional state of an infant, but it does require each of us to listen more carefully than we usually do to how we're feeling at any given time. Before you can actively alter your emotion it's important that you know your own current baseline, so you know if you're ready, and how far you have to go. In addition to listening, a singer must accept the value of openly expressed emotion, which is unfortunately too often seen as weak or inappropriate. A committed singer must then begin to take the time to actively explore emotion. Rather than bury feelings, bring them to the forefront. To become more comfortable expressing emotion in our daily lives (when and where appropriate) is to begin to exercise a muscle that has atrophied in many of us.

Sometimes, in fact often, the feelings are easy, especially if you're in a safe place (as your rehearsal should be) and you're doing something you enjoy (singing alongside people you like). Unless something upsetting has happened recently, your singers should have a comfortable emotional baseline that allows them to be present with their feelings in rehearsal without tapping into something difficult or unpleasant.

We are all complex emotional beings, and throughout our lives we have had many experiences that made a variety of deep impressions upon us. It is possible that some singers have ongoing emotional struggles or suppressed feelings that come to the surface once your group begins to explore certain issues. This is not abnormal, but if the issues appear too large or deep in scope to be handled in rehearsal, it's important that you let the individual know he or she will be best served by seeing a licensed psychologist or psychiatrist who can help him or her unpack and address those feelings. There are too many different scenarios and potential issues to be addressed by this book or anyone who doesn't have years of experience in professional therapy.

Moreover, an emotionally troubled person has the potential to throw a rehearsal out of balance, requiring significant attention or demanding excessive time. Most of us singers are akin to all artists, more emotional and sensitive than the general population, and yet there are limits and levels of control we can exercise to remain within social norms and pull away from the emotion when needed. It should be clear if the rare individual in your group needs to take a break or is not capable of taking various emotional journeys with the rest of your singers.

FACIAL CONNECTEDNESS

I want freedom for the full expression of my personality.
—GANDHI

It's said that only the rarest of individuals are able to lie without being able to be detected by an expert. This is because we all show our feelings on our faces, and it takes an extremely capable actor to deliver a truly believable performance as a completely different person.

Professional stage ensembles, such as those found in Broadway shows or in an opera chorus, are highly adept at pairing superlative acting with harmony singing; for the rest of us, we need to conjure genuine emotion to express genuine emotion. Anything less will be read as false.

We all know singers who are able to put on expressions that are larger than life, and perhaps in a big concert hall the people in the back are convinced; but anyone up close can see that the wide eyes and extreme gestures don't equate to joy, and the furrowed brow doesn't immediately signal an honest intensity. In the same way that we smile honestly with our eyes, many subconscious changes happen in our facial structure when we emote, and other people pick up on these signals even if they don't actively realize that they do.

Great singing with authentic emotional expression does not require acting. Your singers will remain themselves throughout the performance, and the techniques that follow do not take years of professional training to master. Before mastery comes knowledge and understanding, so the next step is to explore the deceptively simple question "What is emotion?"

Emotions

DEFINITION

I adore art . . . when I am alone with my notes,
my heart pounds and the tears stream from my eyes,
and my emotion and my joys are too much to bear.
—Giuseppe Verdi

Defining emotion is more difficult than one might assume. Yes, emotions are feelings, as dictionaries tautologically declare, but what does that actually mean?

Let's start with what we observe: an emotion is a universal, biologically innate state that is expressed to others through facial expressions.[1] The basic facial expressions of emotion don't exist for our own good, because we clearly know our thoughts internally. They evolved over time to allow us to express ourselves and communicate with others.

Yet facial expression may not tell the whole story of our emotions, even to the attentive observer. Studies show that we accurately identify others' emotions based on facial expression only about 58 percent of the time.[2] We know how we feel, and we know

---

1 Even this simple definition of "emotion" is neither comprehensive nor universally agreed upon. Part of the reason for this is historical, as the word "emotion" didn't exist until the 1600s. Ancient Greek and Roman society frowned upon "passions and affections" as standing in contrast to logic, which they believed was the antidote to human suffering—and their influence endured through the ages. Acceptance of emotion in most of today's cultures is greater, not only as a social phenomenon but as the subject of scientific study. For example, in the words of American research psychologist Carroll Izard, "Emotion consists of neural circuits (that are at least partially dedicated), response systems, and a feeling state/process that motivates and organizes cognition and action. Emotion also provides information to the person experiencing it, and may include antecedent cognitive appraisals and ongoing cognition including an interpretation of its feeling state, expressions or social-communicative signals, and may motivate approach or avoidant behavior, exercise control/regulation of responses, and be social or relational in nature." Yet no academic definition has won universal agreement. Fortunately, we don't need to decide on one in order to feel and convey emotion when we sing!

2 Julie Beck, "Hard Feelings: Science's Struggle to Define Emotions," *The Atlantic,* February 24, 2015.

that others share our feelings, but we're not great at identifying a particular emotion from a facial expression alone.

Thankfully, within context we are far better at identifying another's feelings. Context, so vital in movies, dance, art, and music, is no less central to our own lives. A story, a lyric, the interactions between characters: these give an audience the ability to follow along and empathize. As a singer, you can breathe a sigh of relief: your facial expressions don't have to be perfect, and they don't need to be the same from person to person, as we're not terribly good at using facial cues alone to know how another person is feeling. If we're telling a story, if we're engaged, if we're alongside others who are doing the same, more than half the battle is won.

Going deeper, the quest to understand the mechanics of emotion can yield valuable insights for us as performers. In the late 19th century, the James/Lange Theory of Emotion was based on the principle that the physical and chemical changes we undergo in certain situations are perceived in our brains as emotion. If you're camping and you see a bear approaching your tent, your body releases adrenaline, your heart races, your breathing rate increases, and time seems to slow. Our brain connects these various elements and tells us we're feeling fear.

Since then, scientists have rejected the notion that emotions are simply a physical state of being (although in a sense everything we think and do and experience can be distilled to physics—forces pushing on other forces, electrons firing in our brain synapses, and so forth). Yet the knowledge that physical actions can directly influence emotion can help us to unlock honest vocal performances. If you move the corners of your mouth upward into a forced smile, you can actually make yourself happier. This is a kind of physical-emotional therapy that has been studied and proven: smiling makes you happy, just as being happy makes you smile. The book *Presence*, by Amy Cuddy, underlines the similar power of body language and physical posture. To stand in a mirror with legs spread shoulder width and arms akimbo is to increase one's confidence. Our bodies retain a direct connection to, and influence over, our emotional state.[3] This growing body of knowledge can be

---

3 You can experience for yourself how the physical triggers the emotional right now. Punch a pillow, stomp your foot and yell, and you'll start to feel angry. Stand up tall, lift your eyes and cheekbones, smile, and you'll start to feel joy. Obviously, these actions are not without limitations, as chemical depression or just having received great news will flood your body with feelings that you can't

harnessed in your group's stance and choreography to help reinforce your emotional message, both internally, for the singers, and externally, for the audience.

Modern psychological theorists have looked to codify and distill feelings to figure out if some are basic, like primary colors, and others are higher-level, a combination of the core emotions. The result was a list of six core emotions:

- Joy
- Anger
- Fear
- Surprise
- Disgust
- Sadness

If you've seen the animated film *Inside Out*, you'll recognize these core emotions as central elements of the movie. Each individual has five of these (the filmmakers dropped surprise, as they felt five was the right number. It's a Disney Pixar movie, after all, not a PBS special).

The most recent studies on the subject (with titles like "Dynamic Facial Expressions of Emotion Transmit an Evolving Hierarchy of Signals Over Time") have determined that in fact there are only four truly core emotions. Disgust is very closely linked to and develops out of anger as babies age, while surprise is a situational mixture of joy and fear. If the history of music is any indication, the primacy of these four emotions can be confirmed, as disgust and surprise are far less often the subject and core emotional focus of songs.

These remaining four emotions—joy, anger, fear, and sadness—are the building blocks, the primary colors of human emotional experience. We experience them several times a day in different forms, and all of our nuanced emotions and complex, conflicted modern feelings grow from these building blocks. It's important to identify and understand them, each in their own way, to best conjure them in rehearsal and on stage.

On the Lifetime Television reality docuseries *Pitch Slapped*, I was assigned the underdog group, Stay Tuned, from Cherry Hill East High School in Cherry Hill, New Jersey. Their biggest disadvantage

---

simply overcome with a few gestures, but if you're in a neutral emotional state, this process has been proven clinically to work.

was that they were an after-school club, not a class, so they did not have much time throughout the year to grow, bond, and learn as they established a sound and repertoire. When I first met them, I realized that it was essential for me to first teach them how to express honest emotion. To build upon a foundation of technique without emotion was to doom them to a lifetime of thinking that the point of music is notes and rhythms, and that competitions are a kind of vocal-fold Olympics, where nothing matters more than how precisely you execute vocal maneuvers. Win or lose, regardless of the complexity of arrangements or choreography, if they couldn't connect to a song and each other with an emotional power and consistency, there was no chance we could make great music together. I chose their first four songs specifically to focus on each of the four core emotions. I recommend a similar tactic when working with a group that has not considered emotion in music, so you can lay a strong initial groundwork.

JOY

*For me, music-making is the most joyful activity possible,
the most perfect expression of any emotion.*
—LUCIANO PAVAROTTI

Of the four basic emotions, joy is the runaway favorite. There are sections of several industries dedicated to helping people find happiness: through books, therapy, exercise, positive thinking, medication, and so on.[1] It is a universal right, at least for all Americans, as outlined in Thomas Jefferson's oft-quoted phrase "Life, liberty, and the pursuit of happiness." Happiness even has its own day: the United Nations declared March 20 the "International Day of Happiness." Let's hope it helps raise awareness of and sensitivity toward happiness, that most maligned and misunderstood of concepts.

When we sing a joyful song, we need to conjure joy, and yet the techniques espoused above all take time. On stage we don't have time for a workout, nature hike, or 50-minute therapy session. To deliver a joyful song on stage you need to be able to tap into happiness immediately, and then perhaps shift right out of it if the next song is in a very different mood.

For any group, joy should be the easiest emotion to access, as singing is such a joyful activity, and there is an almost unlimited supply of happy songs in all styles of music, appropriate for every level of singer. Some of a cappella's most successful songs of all time have been happy, including the only a cappella song to reach number one on the *Billboard* charts in America: Bobby McFerrin's "Don't Worry, Be Happy."

If you have a group of young singers, you'll likely emphasize this emotion above all others because it's the easiest, and because it can be difficult approaching and dealing with the other emotions at a young age. For older students, you might find that programming too

---

1   Many of the books on happiness make clear a link between volunteerism—giving of many kinds—and a resulting joy, satisfaction, deep happiness. Singing is a gift to an audience and, when approached as such, especially in situations where people are in need, can be deeply rewarding.

many purely happy songs feels cloying or insipid, especially if you have a batch of moody, brooding teenagers. In all cases, just as you match a song to your group's vocal range, age, and style, so should you take emotional appropriateness into consideration.

It's worth noting that joy is perhaps the easiest emotion to sing, but only if given fertile ground. Singers assemble for rehearsal with a million different thoughts in their minds and perhaps tensions in their bodies, which is why some directors like to use physical as well as musical warm-ups, to help people let go of the rest of their day and turn to the task of making music. It can take time to shed the stresses of the day, whether they arise from family, school, work, a near miss on the freeway, or even an unpleasant ride on the subway. By making rehearsal a safe space, and creating effective transitions into rehearsal time, you can help minimize the weight of the outside world on your singers' individual and collective emotional states.

As described in the previous chapter, you and your fellow singers can "jump start" joy by lifting your eyebrows and corners of your mouth: smile. You may find some singers for whom this notion sounds ridiculous (and it may to you as well), and if they're actively or subconsciously sabotaging the process to prove their skepticism correct, then they will likely not have the same success as the rest of the group. However, it has been proven to work well beyond the placebo effect. If approached with an open mind, this simple technique can be a powerful first step.

In addition to muscular triggers, specific syllables in an arrangement can have a direct impact on the group's emotional experience. In 1989, psychologist Robert Zajonc studied the effect of different vowel sounds on mood and learned that a long "e" sound, which places the face in a position close to a smile, made singers feel happier, whereas a dark "oo" vowel, replicating a pout, made singers feel worse. This is not to say that you should never include an "oo" vowel in a happy arrangement, but you should consider shifting some vowels to happier sounds, and if you do have a lot of "oo" in the song, make the vowel a little wider and sing it with a smile.[2]

---

2 This subject has been studied at length from various angles. Putting a pen in your mouth lengthwise, forcing a smile, makes people feel better, and pushing your lips outward, forcing a pout, makes people feel worse. People have made these faces in a mirror alone, or with other people present, and always report the same result. Scientists don't know why it works, but it works, provided you're in an emotionally neutral state.

These tips are not the alpha and omega of joyful singing, only a first step in that direction. There's plenty more to come, once we've considered the nature of the other fundamental human emotions.

ANGER

A wonderful emotion to get things moving when one is stuck is anger.
It was anger more than anything else that had set me off,
roused me into productivity and creativity.
—Mary Garden

nger is an essential emotion, if an unpleasant one at times.
Increased heart rate and blood pressure coupled with adrenaline
prepare us for confrontation and indicate our body's active
response to a threatening situation.

The facial response to anger is perceivable in animals as well as
humans: a wide stance and inflated body size (to show strength),
flared nostrils (to take in more oxygen in preparation for physical
conflict), bared teeth (to indicate a willingness to fight), and an
unblinking stare at the aggressor coupled along with a furrowed
brow (indicating intense focus), all in hopes of making the other
acquiesce. Verbal cues are also equated with anger, from growls to
barks, indicating one's heightened state and unwillingness to back
down. These features are seen throughout the animal kingdom as
well as in toddlers worldwide, indicating they are innate, nature as
opposed to the result of nurture.

It's clear why we experience anger, but why do we sing about
anger? Catharsis. The process of experiencing and releasing anger in
art can be positive and creative, whereas unbridled anger in other
situations may prove destructive. This is why we are drawn to listen
to angry music as well, to stir up and release feelings, to allow us to
feel connected to others who are angry, perhaps for the same reason.
Rock and roll music was born of rebellion and anger and will always
have a new audience as teenagers rebel against their parents, school,
society, and pretty much everything else. As James Dean famously
said in *Rebel Without a Cause*, "What have you got?"[1]

Songs of rebellion against one's elders and authority are a

---

1 If you're working with teenagers, righteous indignation offers easy access to anger
for most if not all of your singers. Although it's about her divorce rather than
social injustice, Pink's "So What" provided the perfect platform for Stay Tuned,

staple in every era and can be found in almost every style of music. Even folk music, that dulcet marriage of vocal harmonies and acoustic roots instruments, was the soundtrack to much of the protest movement in the early 1960s. And if you think classical choral music is all sweetness and light, you haven't sung "O Fortuna" from Orff's *Carmina Burana*. In other words, anger can be found everywhere.

When singing, several elements can help reinforce anger, the most obvious being a loud dynamic marking. Of course, an angry song will not always be fortissimo throughout, so in quiet passages, staccato phrasing and sharp, crisp consonants will indicate continued intensity. Precise enunciation, perhaps bordering on over-enunciation, throughout all dynamic levels can reflect a heightened state and aggressive nature.

Physiologically, disgust has been categorized under the umbrella of anger, as researchers have found the two to be indistinguishable during human development. For example, a wrinkled nose is your natural response to "stationary danger" such as a harmful gas. Scientists believe that with the act of wrinkling your nose you're less likely to breathe in dangerous pathogens. Whereas disgust won't occur often in a lyric, there are times in popular music when it comes in handy (TLC's "No Scrubs" comes to mind).

---

culminating in the ultimate iconic act of rock and roll: smashing a guitar on stage. Who says instrumentalists should have all the fun?

FEAR

I am not fearless. I get scared plenty.
But I have also learned how to channel that emotion to sharpen me.
—BEAR GRYLLS

Fear, the other half of the "fight or flight" equation, served our ancestors very well in helping them assess their ability to face an immediate threat. Unlike anger, which threatens and often results in confrontation, fear would likely trigger avoidance or escape. Fears can be rational or irrational (phobias), but the physiological changes in the body are the same: increased breathing rate (increased oxygen, useful in fleeing), increased heart rate (greater blood circulation to the muscles, also useful in fleeing), hair follicle tension (goose bumps, thought to have initially evolved so as to make a furry frightened animal appear larger), sweating (in anticipation of the increased body heat likely to result from fleeing), increased blood glucose (fast energy), quick awakening if asleep, and the like.

Throughout the animal kingdom, insects, birds, fish, reptiles, and mammals all emit pheromones to alarm other members of the same species. Although a substance of this nature has not been fully identified and studied in humans, if it exists it is quite possible that a room full of singers feeling fearful would signal the audience via these odorless alarm substances, which would be a powerful effect (this may be why people enjoy watching a scary movie in a full as opposed to empty theater).

Some people experience periodic or chronic anxiety, which is linked to fear but distinct, as fear is a reaction to a situation demanding a choice, often imminent, whereas anxiety presents itself in the face of unavoidable circumstances, where flight is not possible.

Of the four core emotions, fear is by far the least frequently referenced in popular music, although a few notable songs do exist, such as "Enter Sandman," "Somebody's Watching Me," and "The Fear." Perhaps it is because the sound of a human voice is reassuring that horror movie soundtracks rely on synthesizers and tremolo strings to underscore creaky stairs and moonless forests. In fact, there are likely more songs in existence imploring people to not be fearful ("Don't Fear the Reaper," "I Hope You Dance," "I Won't Back Down," "Not Afraid") than those that immerse the listener in a fearful mood. Nonetheless, with fear as a component of other, more complex moods, it's good to be able to draw upon it when needed.

Surprise is closely linked to fear, with many of the same physiological symptoms but a few differences, including raised eyebrows, open eyelids, dilated pupils (wide-open eyes, taking in as much information as possible quickly about potential fast-approaching danger), and the resulting wrinkled forehead. The primary difference between fear and surprise is that of time: with surprise, there is an immediacy that comes from being startled, from a situation that happens too quickly to be fully processed all at once, so the body is overloaded and the fear mechanism is triggered just in case. Unlike fear, surprise doesn't always have a negative underpinning, as the end result of the unexpected moment might be a good one (like a surprise party . . . if you like surprise parties). Following the initial flood of chemicals, we experience a feeling of relief, much as if we're watching a movie of an event as opposed to actually in significant danger.[1]

Feelings of fear and surprise can be conjured through several different musical techniques: juxtaposition (quiet then loud, fast then slow, silence then sound), a quickening pace, crescendo, increased rhythmic intensity, and anything else that signals an increase, the approach of danger. All of these can be found in John Williams' brilliant score to the movie *Jaws*, with a theme that starts very quietly and very low, just a minor second, then a long pause, then a repeat, and a slow build until the entire orchestra is fully engaged.

---

1 One of the great musical jokes of all time is Haydn's Symphony No. 94, better known as the "Surprise" Symphony. The second movement is well known, with its tiptoeing staccato melody followed by a giant orchestral thud. Though you may not know the piece by name, if you search for it online, you'll likely find that you know it from a cartoon, commercial, or some other source—and, now that you know what to expect, it'll likely make you smile.

SADNESS

Give sorrow words; the grief that does not speak knits up
the o'erwrought heart and bids it break.
—SHAKESPEARE

Along with joy, sadness is the emotion most often represented in music. For every happy love song, there's a ballad about heartache, love lost, failed relationships.

Sadness is a very powerful emotional subject for a song because of its very nature. As explained in the film *Inside Out*, the expression of feelings of loss, despair, helplessness, and sorrow elicits feelings of empathy in others, and it is this connection that inspires our family, friends, and community to help us.

Sadness is unique among the four core emotions, as it is the one that most people try to avoid. People want happy endings, which has been proven for decades in Hollywood. Can you imagine *Pretty Woman* being as popular if Richard Gere drove off at the end, leaving Julia Roberts sobbing in the street, as was originally intended? *Little Shop of Horrors* ending with the plant eating everyone, as director Frank Oz wanted? *National Lampoon's Vacation* ending with Roy Walley entertaining the family at gunpoint in his own home as the film originally ended (the ending we know was reshot six months after wrap when test audiences hated this darker ending)? *Pretty in Pink* with Andie ending up with her buddy Duckie instead of Blane, the heartthrob she (and test audiences) preferred? People also seek out anger, especially athletes, who want the adrenaline to motivate them. And of course horror films are a very popular segment of the film business, with audiences tolerating bad special effects, cheesy dialogue, and bad acting if they're sufficiently frightened.

We do sometimes turn to sad songs in times of sadness. When we're feeling bad, they help us process our feelings, make us feel connected to the musicians, help us realize we're not alone in feeling this way and that in time the situation and feeling will pass. Perhaps we sometimes enjoy listening to sad songs when we're not feeling sad because they are a reminder of how we might but don't feel, a window into the darker side of someone else's soul as we remain safe at a distance.

Sadness has several physical characteristics, including slumped shoulders, lowered gaze, downturned mouth, low energy, and ultimately tears. Unlike the other emotions, which increase the body's size or openness in different ways, sorrow triggers a physical diminution as one looks inward and retreats from the world. When we feel sad, we don't feel like going anywhere or doing anything. For this reason, elaborate choreography isn't appropriate, and often the best choice is to stand and deliver. In this case, less is more. Draw people in, just as sadness itself creates a connection with others and draws them to you.

EMOTIONAL COMPLEXITY

A film is—or should be—more like music than like fiction.
It should be a progression of moods and feelings. The theme,
what's behind the emotion, the meaning, all that comes later.
—STANLEY KUBRICK

nger, fear, joy, sadness: all are considered basic emotions because they are automatically triggered, based on our immediate
situation, and are present in all people in all cultures at a very
early age. But what about more nuanced feelings like shame, guilt,
or pride? These emotions are more complex because they require a
measure of self-reflection and self-evaluation, the result of circumstance and thought.

Consider shame and embarrassment, which at first glance may
appear to be the same. They differ due to one's understanding
of the situation; guilt results from a major moral transgression,
embarrassment from a social gaffe. Embarrassment only exists in
terms of a social setting, as you can't be embarrassed if no one saw
you, whereas guilt can weigh heavily on someone's heart even if
no one else knows about your actions. You can laugh off an embarrassing moment, but guilt is no laughing matter.

Some emotions can be understood as a marriage of primary
emotions, just as you can make orange by mixing yellow and red.
The feeling of wonder, perhaps as experienced when first enter-
ing the chocolate room in Willy Wonka's factory or seeing the
Christmas tree grow from six feet to six stories tall in a live production of *The Nutcracker*, can be understood to be a mixture of joy
and surprise. Some other emotions can be best understood as the
opposites of other emotions, the way that pride is the opposite of
shame, one's self-reflection on good deeds.

As we are complex beings, there is no limit to the combinations
of circumstances and nuance that inform our emotions. Part of the
interest we find in literature and other great long-form art is the
creation of complex emotions, resulting from hundreds of pages
of circumstance and backstory. It would be impossible to render a

complete list of emotions here, as there is no single agreed-upon list. If you want a list, it's better that you start your own, although the more you strive to understand and categorize emotion, the better you'll see the challenges that face modern social scientists. To truly understand ourselves and others emotionally there is no single formula, no easy equation, no comprehensive list. We must look inward and outward to understand the complexities of each situation, and through careful analysis find each song's true meaning. But before we can analyze a song, we need to decide what song we're singing, and how it should be sung.

Choices

APPROPRIATENESS

The first principle of architectural beauty
is that the essential lines of a construction be determined
by a perfect appropriateness to its use.
—GUSTAVE EIFFEL

People often ask, "Can any song be sung a cappella?" and my response is, "Yes, but not every song can be sung well by every group." Matching the song to the group is essential, as you want to make sure your group has the necessary character, vocal range, lead singer (if applicable), and so on.

Of course, emotion ranks among these key considerations. Just as you consider whether the lyrics of a song are appropriate for a young group, so too should you consider whether the emotions are. If you're working with middle schoolers, you'll likely find them timid about sharing difficult emotions. It's probably safest to start with songs centered on joy, and work outward toward other emotions if your singers appear ready. If you have a choir that includes several veterans, you might find anger and fear to be challenging emotions to tackle, potentially triggering PTSD symptoms. Then again, that might be exactly the right direction for such a choir, if the members are open and they're eager to sing about their own powerful experiences.

In all cases, it makes sense to start by establishing easier themes, later expanding your repertoire to include more potentially overwhelming emotions. Use your judgment and taste, and if you are uncertain, tread lightly and talk with members of the group to get a sense of their feelings about a song or mood.

SONG

Words make you think. Music makes you feel.
A song makes you feel a thought.
—E. Y. HARBURG

When it comes to choosing music for your vocal harmony group, the options are endless. You could spend a lifetime searching and never hear all of them. Yet your rehearsal hours are limited, and you don't have time to try a lot of random music just to see what sticks. When you choose a song, you need to know it's the right one.

And what is the right one? Above all, the choice should be based on emotion. A director will usually look at the highest and lowest notes and the overall difficulty of a piece, but that is only one dimension, and not the most important one, as notes can be changed. Start with the big picture in mind: What emotions can your group best express? What message(s) can they deliver? Obviously, young singers can sing about being young and black singers about being black, but you can go deeper. There are additional layers of common experience, community, and belief that likely provide you with rich soil in which to plant your musical statements.

If you have not done this before, start with the emotions and messages that are most central to your group's purpose and character, the low-hanging fruit. Once you have those songs mastered, it is time to venture beyond the obvious and see how you might stretch yourselves, building upon these core strengths and making song selections that will begin to expand your group's palette of emotional color and breadth.

Of course, in some songs the group's emotional presentation takes a back seat to one individual, in which case you need to make sure you have the right person to act as emotional centerpiece and focus, delivering the song's lead vocal.

SOLO

Never tell me the odds.
—HAN SOLO

We love the lone hero, the protagonist who succeeds despite great odds. More books and movies have been written about individuals than any other subject, and with good reason: we like to identify with them, particularly those whose plights and struggles are in some way parallel to or informative of our own. It is no different in the field of music, which is why we are drawn to hearing a story told, a melody sung by a single person.

If it is important that your group be able to relate to and deliver a song with emotional honesty, it's doubly important that the mood and message of a solo resonate with the soloist. Just as most people can't convincingly say something that they don't truly believe, most singers are incapable of delivering a solo that is not something they can relate to or empathize with. It's not essential that the lyrics of a song express the exact feelings or experiences of your soloist (we'll address how to do this later), but it is necessary that your soloist be able to empathize and feel the song's mood and message. Just as I like to remind people that any song can be sung a cappella but not every group can sing every song, there are songs that people can effectively sing and songs they can't effectively sing, and it's more about heart than vocal range.

On the flip side, there is definitely a solo for everyone, every person on this planet. As we've already discussed, some of the most successful musicians, like Bob Dylan, Tom Waits, and Billie Holiday, have voices that are far from traditional. Many other popular singers, like Britney Spears, Paula Abdul, and Madonna, have built their success chiefly on their dancing and their personality on and off stage, making their voices secondary. If there's a person in your group whom you want to have deliver a solo, look for the right emotional fit first and foremost, then figure out how to resolve issues of vocal range and the like based on the song's overall presentation.

PRESENTATION

It usually takes me three weeks to prepare a good impromptu speech.
—MARK TWAIN

We've all seen it happen, and likely experienced it from the stage: the way a song is presented can make or break it. Great songs have been ruined with silly choreography, and yet thoughtful staging, lights, wardrobe, and the like can give the audience chills. This being the case, why wait until a song is learned before considering the way your group will deliver it to the audience?

The way you're presenting a song can go as deep as the song's mood, or as high as high concept. For example, let's imagine a group is singing "I Feel Pretty" from *West Side Story*. The first choice you have to make is: are you performing it in earnest, or are you sending it up? Will it be sweet and beautiful, or silly and over the top? Or perhaps you want to use the song to make a point about feminism, sexuality, objectification. It could be sung angrily; it could be a joyful, campy romp with guys in dresses. I mention all of these possibilities for just one song before we move on to analysis because these kinds of decisions so greatly alter the nature of your performance that they can move the song in or out of the "we should sing this" column.

Also, don't make the mistake of being overly earnest, especially upon finishing this book. Like all educational processes, it is possible to swing too far in a certain direction and, although you'll correct yourself in time, I'd like to save you the trouble. What do I mean? Let's take a song like "Bohemian Rhapsody," by Queen. It's a classic, a fevered nightmare, episodic, with different tempos and styles, all gloriously presented in the original. How should you perform the song? Upon closing this book, you may find yourself analyzing each passage and assigning emotions: fear, anger . . . wait a minute. Yes, there's an element of fear, and yes, there's anger, but I don't want you to lose the forest for the trees. Ultimately, this song is larger than life, somewhat campy, and fun. When sung with a wink it comes alive—but if sung completely earnestly, it could collapse under its own sense of self-importance. This is what I am saying: don't take everything too seriously, don't always try to make a statement or be emotionally heavy. With apologies to Freud, sometimes an over-the-top seventies rock anthem is just an over-the-top seventies rock anthem.

With that in mind, take a broad view. Maybe there's a song you'd love to do, but it just isn't going to work for your group in a straightforward way. Okay, but is there a nontraditional, clever angle? A send-up? A parody? Perhaps you alter the tempo significantly, the groove, the feel, the mood. At this point, you're beginning to consider the arrangement.

ARRANGEMENT

Art is a process of delivering or arranging elements
that appeal to the emotions of a person looking at it. It's what you feel.
—SHAQUILLE O'NEAL

Unlike a garage band that can strum chords without ever having written down a note, vocal harmony groups require an arrangement, usually written, especially if there is more than one person singing each voice part. Who will sing what, when, must be determined, as the human voice is not polyphonic.[1]

"Vocal translation" is the usual first step for beginning arrangers, who tend to exert most of their creative energies figuring out how to translate the instrumental parts into vocal parts. Textural creativity comes next, as arrangers begin to explore other ways to present a song with voices, while still preserving the overall feel, key, and tempo of the original versions. In time, arrangers learn to trust their instincts to the point that they can break the original song's mold and present a song in a completely different style, format, key, tempo, and form.

Whether or not you're arranging for your group, you should be making your arranging choices based on the emotional heart of your song choice and the character of your soloist and presentation. Even if you're not an arranger, you can and in fact should arrange. The notes on the page are guidelines, a road map to help your group connect to the audience. If you have a way to connect that is better than what's written, then change what's written. Do not be shy; do not be concerned with the arranger's feelings. I am an arranger and I urge groups to change my arrangements. Think of the sheet music as a suit off the rack at a department store, and you're a tailor who can make every piece of fabric custom-fit your

---

1 I will concede that one can sing a note and whistle another, and some overtone singers are able to create a significantly pronounced overtone. However, these techniques are difficult, limited in scope, and only rarely used in vocal harmony compositions and arrangements. For almost all practical purposes, the human voice alone is monophonic.

singers. Wouldn't you? Shouldn't you? Absolutely. The music belongs to you, so make it your own.

What should you change? Anything at all that will make the song more emotionally impactful: notes, rhythms, dynamics, syllables, key, form, you name it. Your guiding star should always be clear: how do I get these singers (and that soloist, if there is one) to make this song the perfect conduit for these emotions, this feeling, this moment? How can I make this melody soar, these lyrics come to life? Don't sing *forte* just because it's written in the music; sing *forte* because the music compels you to, because that's what feels right. Question everything, and experiment as you learn. See what happens naturally when your singers are focused and engaged, breathing life into the song's meaning.

Meanings

DEPTH

Words mean more than what is set down on paper.
It takes the human voice to infuse them with shades of deeper meaning.
—Maya Angelou

There is great power in our voices when we sing, just as there is when we speak. When we express ourselves to a family member or friend, we're fully present or, as some say, "in the moment," thoroughly focused on sharing ideas and recalling experiences, all with an emotional context and subtext. With the exception of the occasional automatic "How's it going?" or "Thanks," when we speak, the words that come out of our mouth reflect the emotions and thoughts we are feeling at that exact moment.

Since a group of people is unlikely to be feeling the same thing at the same time, or to express their feelings identically, we turn to written music with lyrics to communally express.

This may not have occurred to you before. You have been drawn to music because you like the feeling that it gives you, the feeling you get when you create music with other people, and the experience of sharing it with an audience. With rare exception singing is not something we do primarily because it's financially lucrative or otherwise significantly beneficial in the way that a chore or job is. We do it because we love it.

However, for it to work as it is intended, for the music and mood and meaning to come to life, we need to move beyond our own experience in the moment and connect with others through a song to simultaneously share a feeling as we create harmony. There is inherent beauty in the chords we sing, but that is not enough. The various elements of music exist to serve a greater purpose: to express a thought, an experience, a feeling.

Every song has meaning, yet that meaning is not always spelled out. Some lyrics run deep, and performers or even songwriters can conjure emotion without having consciously analyzed the song. On the other hand, some topics and themes are so universal that they don't require conversation. "Oh, What a Beautiful Morning" is so straightforward, so clear, that everyone understands the mood and implication of the song.

But to expect such serendipitous emotional unity throughout your entire repertoire is foolish (as you likely realize, since you're reading this book). As much as possible, the subconscious should become conscious, and the personal communal. Some people shy away from emotions, others never analyze lyrics, but without it a singing group is doomed to, at best, intermittently stumble upon powerful emotional moments in all but the most obvious songs.

The first step to understanding a song is to take it at face value: analyze the lyrics.

LYRICAL ANALYSIS

When you are describing
A shape, or sound, or tint;
Don't state the matter plainly,
But put it in a hint;
And learn to look at all things.
With a sort of mental squint.
—Lewis Carroll

There is no single proper methodology you should follow to understand lyrics, nor is there always a single popular interpretation of a song's fundamental meaning. Throughout human history, writers have written, readers and listeners have analyzed, and sometimes audiences arrive at a different meaning than even the writer intended. Don't think lyricists always have all the answers, as some songs, like novels, can carry meanings that are not clear to the writer and take time to fully understand.

In addition, we can look at lyrics from another time and often learn something about the culture that the author never intended. Much of who we are, what we believe, and how we act is determined by a number of cultural precepts and social mores of which we are likely unaware. In a few hundred years people will look at the lyrics of our popular music and find in it clues to our culture the way we can look at lyrics from ancient Greece, the Civil War, or the 1960s and understand the time and culture with a removed and perhaps more objective clarity.

There are many tools you can use when analyzing a lyric that will help you approach the text from a variety of perspectives. These help unlock a number of the most common narrative techniques found in all forms of writing, especially literary fiction:

- What is the song's apparent subject matter? Is it straightforward or layered? *(allegory, metaphor)*

- What's the apparent meaning? Is there likely another level of meaning beneath it? *(theme)*
- Is the song a moment or a journey? Do things change or remain the same?
- If the lyrics describe a story or some kind of change, what is the change? Are things better at the end? Was any conflict resolved? Was justice served?
- Is the sense of time clear in the song, or does it shift? *(backstory, foreshadowing, flash forward)*
- Who is the narrator? How does this person fit into the story/ moment? *(first, second, or third person)* Is the story her own? *(surrogate narrator)* Are there additional characters? What are their relationships? Who is the narrator addressing?
- What are the narrator's feelings? *(pathos)* Is the listener meant to share those feelings? Are they straightforward? *(satire, irony, parody)*
- Do you believe the narrator is telling you the truth, the whole truth, and nothing but the truth? *(unreliable narrator, hyperbole)*
- What is the context of the lyric? Are there any social or histori-cal considerations? Any events in the lyricist's life to take into account?
- Do you understand all of the words? The grammar? Is it pos-sible some of the words have double or multiple meanings?
- Is the language used common, slang, formal, archaic, poetic?
- Does the title further inform your analysis in any way?
- Are there any musical elements that reveal anything about the lyric, intellectually or emotionally? *(use of motif, text painting)*
- How does this lyric translate to and speak to our current time and culture?
- Is the song either overtly or covertly religious? How does the religion inform the above points?

. . . and this is not an exhaustive list. As with a mystery, you should follow loose ends until you find the answer, or determine that it's not ultimately knowable.

Rather than fill these pages with lyrical analysis, I leave you to tackle this process with songs that are meaningful to you and songs that your group is singing. You are not alone in this task, as multiple web sites exist to help you on your quest to better understand a lyric.[1] Songmeanings.com and lyricinterpretations.com are two that exist as of the publication of this book, and as with all things online you can expect web sites to come and go. You can also find web sites devoted to a single songwriter or album, such as thewallanalysis.com, which dissects Pink Floyd's iconic concept album. A web search should bring up at least one site for classic popular songs. As for songs that are obscure or were just released, you may be on your own, but that isn't necessarily a bad thing. Your personal interpretation of the lyric is ultimately what matters most, as you'll be the one singing it.

---

1   Traditionally, all of the words in a single song are "a lyric." The plural "lyrics" should refer to the words of multiple songs (e.g., "Paul Simon's lyrics are . . ."), but in common parlance it has come to refer to a single song as well, as in "music and lyrics by. . . ." Nowadays either is fine, but if you want to sound especially learned you may find yourself making statements like: "John Lennon's 'Imagine'? Now that's a great lyric!"

CONTEXT

No word is absolutely wrong or dirty or insulting.
It all depends upon context and intention.
—JANET JACKSON

There is often a broad historical context for songs that reach beyond individual relationships. "Right Here, Right Now," by Jesus Jones, makes far more sense when you understand it in the context of the time it was written. It can certainly be sung about other time periods, perhaps ironically if the repurposed historical context is intentionally a negative one. Joni Mitchell's "Woodstock" and Gordon Lightfoot's "The Wreck of the Edmund Fitzgerald" are very clearly about specific historical events, which you should absolutely research and understand to effectively perform them.

There isn't always a specific social context for a song, but when there is it is often powerful. On the other hand, a lyric that is fairly open to interpretation can also capture the spirit of an age, as in Sam Cooke's "A Change Is Gonna Come" or Bob Dylan's "The Times, They Are A-Changin'." It is difficult to fully understand a socially relevant lyric without looking at what was happening in society while the song was being written. Some songs from other eras, when heard now, will have a very different resonance with the listener. "Keep Young and Beautiful," "Lollipops and Roses," and "Wives and Lovers" are just a few songs from the past that will strike contemporary listeners as fundamentally sexist, allowing you to make a statement the songwriters clearly never intended.

A song may also have a very personal context, as its meaning comes from moments in a songwriter's life. Billy Joel's "Lullabye" has a poignant lyric, promising the listener that he will never leave her, which is doubly powerful when you learn that he wrote it for his daughter while in the middle of a divorce. The words were not just a thought experiment. They were immediate, meaningful, laden with the complex feelings that accompany such upheaval and the fears with which parents and children anticipate separation.

There may also be intentionally obscured meanings in a lyric. Before gay rights were publicly accepted, Cole Porter wrote songs like "You'd Be So Nice to Come Home To" and "(You'd Be) So Easy to Love" about men he loved but had to offer them as love songs between men and women. This doesn't mean the songs can't be sung by heterosexuals or be given other contexts, but it is important to know their origin, as it lends poignancy and at times additional meaning to some lyrics.

Sometimes people disagree over the meaning of a song, and that too lends another layer to a song. "Puff, the Magic Dragon" and "Bridge Over Troubled Water" are thought to be songs about illicit drugs, as is "Lucy in the Sky with Diamonds." Whether or not the rumors about these songs are true, their prevalence may inform your performance choices (wardrobe, lighting, etc.). Moreover, knowing these popular interpretations can spare you an embarrassing gaffe, such as singing "Bridge Over Troubled Water" at an anti-drug rally, which could result in the local press skewering you for your ignorance.

The more you know about a song, the better you are able to decide the layers of meaning it will have for you and your fellow singers and avoid potentially embarrassing misinterpretations.[1]

It's also valuable to listen to multiple recordings, as different artists' musical and emotional interpretations of a song can provide additional insight into possible readings of the lyric as well as ideas for your arrangement. Some songs, like "Yesterday," by the Beatles, have literally thousands of different versions, so it's obviously not possible to listen to them all, but you can easily skip through several in iTunes, pausing on the ones that appeal to you or provide a unique interpretation.

Perhaps more important than any other meaning is the mean-

---

1   I recall becoming incensed while listening to a group's a cappella rendition of Randy Newman's "Sail Away," one of his most poignant songs. Sung from the point of view of a slave ship captain, the song waxes poetic about the glory of America that the free immigrants will soon enjoy, which of course is the exact opposite of a newly arrived slave's experience. The song hinges on the line "Climb aboard, little wog, sail away with me," as before this it's not clear to whom the song is being sung.

The a cappella group version is sung as a light, finger-snapping pop tune, and they change "little wog" to "little one," apparently oblivious to the song's meaning. A subsequent conversation with the group confirmed my suspicion. Six years later and I'm still angry when I think about it. Sometimes a lovely tune is used to deliver a sinister lyric to great effect. So, before you decide to do a catchy mambo version of "Strange Fruit," you'd better know what kind of fruit the song is about.

ing a song has to you, the listener and potential future performer. Sometimes a lyric's meaning is overt, sometimes it's shrouded in mystery, sometimes it has great historical or social context, and other times it's timeless. What matters most is how the song lands on your ears, and what it means to you. Many a songwriter doesn't like to discuss a song's meaning, in part because it's very personal, and in part because they don't want to cloud your own interpretation. The emotion is likely closely tied to the songwriter's intent, but a cloudy lyric leaves room for you to fill it with your own context, your own personal history.

Once you've studied the lyrics for meaning and context, bring them to your group and see if they agree, and if they're able to bring additional perspective to bear.

GROUP DISCUSSION

A lively discussion is usually helpful,
because the hottest fire makes the hardest steel.
—TOM CLANCY

Beyond the songwriter's intentions, most lyrics have layers of meaning informed by the song's place in the culture. For this reason, lyrics and music alone, without insight, cannot be expected to create a consistent emotional bond between singer and audience. Lyrics must be understood, and if more than one singer is performing them, lyrics must be discussed.

What does this discussion look like?

In the same way that you speak to middle-schoolers differently than adults, and you address a room full of people differently than you speak to a few of your friends, the age, size, and experience of a group will determine in large part the appropriate way to discuss the emotional content of a song.

First of all, how sensitive is the topic? If it's not sensitive at all, you can dive in at any time, or toss out bits of knowledge and insight as you go. This can keep the music interesting, and also save people from being overwhelmed. If you're singing the Beatles' "A Day in the Life" or Don McLean's "American Pie," you're likely better off addressing the lyrics by section as you go, or you might get mired in a 30-minute lecture, much of which will be forgotten by the time you reach Albert Hall or the levee.

Secondly, how complex is the topic? If it's simple, a full-blown discussion might not need to take place. Considering "Walking on Sunshine," by Katrina and the Waves, a few words will likely suffice to express how the song is about love, and the feeling is joy. Nothing deep, nothing complex, just a happy song from start to finish.

On the other hand, if the lyrics are poetic, the song obtuse, the meanings layered, you will likely want to set aside some time to analyze the song with the group. Don't enter this discussion unprepared, as you'll waste precious rehearsal time. Do your research, know what others say the song means, and have your own interpretation (if unique or personal). You should know, at least in broad strokes, what you would like your group's version of the song's emotional message to be, as you shouldn't have chosen the song in the first place if you're not sure there's a good marriage with your group's character and a clear musical path forward. A director should not leave the song's meaning up to an open-ended discussion, unless you're doing a composition by another member of the group (who can better describe what it means than you can), or the song's meaning has many interpretations and your group is small enough that you can quickly agree on a common vision before proceeding.

For everyone else, enter the discussion prepared, perhaps with printed copies of annotated lyrics (or a way to project them so everyone can see) to keep the discussion moving forward efficiently. Touch on the key points and make sure it's all clear as far as you are able (as some songs' lyrical descriptions and mysteries will remain unsolved). Don't worry about complete unanimity, as not every person needs to agree on every detail so long as the emotional shape is communally accepted.

Although you may be rightly concerned about opening a can of worms, a director presenting a song to a larger ensemble or chorus should welcome some input. It's beneficial to hear other interpretations and perspectives, should any arise, especially those of a personal nature. A good director will know which members can speak concisely, and likely be able to read body language and facial expressions to pick out some powerful comments, which will help all of your singers begin to understand the song's message as their own. This said, opening the floor for a protracted, ongoing discussion will significantly erode your rehearsal time. Gather a few opinions; then, unless they undermine your thesis and direction, absorb them and move on to integrating the emotion into the performance.

Before you bring the song to your group for discussion, you should have a good understanding of the song's meaning, how your group will be interpreting it, and what changes (if any) the arrangement makes or will make to the nature of the original. Every one of your technical decisions—including tempo, dynamics, key, feel, style, etc.—should be made with the song's meaning and emotional content in mind.

As you progress, you may find yourself wanting and perhaps needing to make changes to the arrangement so as to have your performance of it maximize the emotional impact. Directors regularly change notes, chords, and rhythms for a variety of reasons (vocal range, technical proficiency of the group, personal taste), and making sure the song's impact is powerful and consistent is as valid a reason as any. Remember that an arrangement is merely a road map, dots and squiggles on a page, to help you convey a piece of music—a feeling, a story, a thought—to the audience. Just as you can take a different road to get to your destination by car, you can take a different path musically.

I have arranged more than 2,000 songs. I consider my arranging central to my persona as a musician; I think I make excellent choices when arranging; and yet none of that matters. I urge directors to change my arrangements all the time, and assure them that I would change them as well were I in the rehearsal. Just as no piece of clothing off the rack fits every person as well as a custom-tailored suit would, so should a piece of music be custom-tailored to suit the voices, style, and persona of a vocal group.[1]

Even if you're struggling with a composition, remember that arrangements of compositions have been happening since before music was first notated. Experiment, tweak, nudge, and settle on the notes and rhythms that work best for your ensemble. Ravel orchestrated Mussorgsky to great effect, and Glenn Gould's performance of Bach was lauded for its originality, even as purists were complaining that it went too far. The Swingle Singers brought legions of new fans to classical music with their jazzy scat interpretations. Music needs to breathe and grow over time to remain relevant to new generations.

As for when you should discuss the song with your group, that can vary based on the group, the song, the rehearsal schedule, and the amount of time you have to work on it before your first performance. Working from generalities, more experienced groups and vocal bands as well as smaller ensembles benefit from knowing what the song means and deciding on the group's interpretation before getting too far in the note-learning process. As these are the kinds of ensembles that tend to incorporate more group member input and feedback, it's best to bring singers into the process early on rather than make changes later based on the group's desired reinterpretation.

---

1 I realize I just made this point a couple of chapters ago, but I feel the need to stress it again because so many directors are reluctant to change music. If you are making decisions for a reason, your choices are more valid than those of the arranger and take precedence because you have more information—namely, you know how you're interpreting the song and what your singers can best do. I promise not to bring this up again if you promise to not hesitate when it's time to tweak an arrangement, okay?

Larger ensembles, choirs, and younger singers are likely in a setting where their director by necessity is telling them what to do at each turn regarding phrasing, dynamics, intensity, and so forth, so the discussion can come later in the process. Once a group of young singers knows their notes and is sounding good, they're usually ready to understand what it all means. As for a large choir, you'll likely not have the time needed to get a great deal of input from all of the singers, so the director can choose an appropriate time to begin working with interpretation. For example, one can address lyrics and topics as they arise. As you move to a new passage, explain what is happening emotionally as well as musically, so both aspects are fresh and intertwined in your singers' minds.

It should go without mentioning that there are certain topics, certain memories, certain emotional issues that some people will not feel comfortable discussing. So long as it's clear they're understanding the process, there is no reason to call anyone out or make anyone share who is remaining quiet. Hopefully the director can tell the difference between members who are avoiding the discussion because they're uncomfortable with emotions and need a little gentle nudging, and those who are fully engaged in the discussion but are intentionally keeping the specifics personal.

And then, unfortunately, in some groups there will be the skeptics, the naysayers. Sometimes individuals who are uncomfortable with emotion will over-intellectualize the lyric and challenge your interpretation so as to allow them to remain in thought rather than feeling. Hopefully they can become engaged in emotional singing in their own way without disrupting the group process by complaining or disagreeing. If not, take them aside, and explain that the task of getting everyone to emote is best served by a public process like this, and all constructive ideas are welcome, but one on one, in private, so as not to undermine the process. These people may have their own way of arriving at an emotional performance, and that's okay, but it is not acceptable for anyone to shame or tease anyone away from open emotional singing. Even an eye roll or heavy sigh can affect the energy in the room, and your introverted singers may be more afraid of peer judgment than you realize. In the end, so long as everyone understands the importance of emotion and delivers on stage, it does not matter how they get there, but it does matter if some members are quashing openness.

Once you and your group have a firm understanding of the lyric, it's time to put your analysis to work.

Perspectives

LIVING THE SONG

Your living is determined not so much by what life brings to you
as by the attitude you bring to life; not so much by what happens to you
as by the way your mind looks at what happens.
—KHALIL GIBRAN

You've analyzed the lyric and figured out the "who, what, when, where, why" of the song; now it's time to embody the "who." What does that mean? Each time you sing a lyric, you should be the "who" at the center of the song, bringing the words to life. To do this, first of all you must believe what you are singing. Just as an actor who is speaking her lines must say them as though they're being said for the first time, a natural reaction to her character's immediate circumstance, so does a singer need to bring truth and immediacy to every word. The difference is that as a singer you don't need to act. You're not someone else: you're you.

However, this doesn't mean you'll always be *you* right now, in this place, in this state of mind. To be able to sing any song you'll sometimes need to leave the present, or assume someone else's perspective.

Before going any further, it's important that you are aware that not everyone can or should sing every song. There are obvious deep divisions that keep some people from singing some songs— e.g., an orthodox Jew may be uncomfortable singing a Christmas carol—and other mismatches that may not be as obvious but can similarly undermine a song's efficacy. Unless you're making a statement rife with detached irony, most children cannot sing songs about being an adult. Most men can't sing "(You Make Me Feel Like a) Natural Woman" unless they're trying to be funny or honestly identify as women. Mismatches abound, you should be wary of choosing a song simply because you like it. You need to be able to make it your own in some way, from some perspective, or else your version will lose what made the original so believable and compelling. To be clear: you don't have to have experienced everything within a song, but you do have to believe it all.

If you're having difficulty understanding this concept, imagine the lyrics as a speech, a series of words you'll deliver to an auditorium full of people. Are you comfortable doing this? Do the words say something real that you can stand behind, even if they're not your own exact experience? For example, as a pacifist you might be able to read some accounts or letters from soldiers in recent wars because they reflect your own perspective or shed light on issues you think important. Other tales from soldiers may strike you as problematic or even offensive. Would you be comfortable delivering them to a crowd? If not then you shouldn't sing them in a song.[1]

Once you have chosen a song that speaks to you and that you will be able to deliver as your own, you should consider whether you can sing it as yourself, just as you are now; whether it's a song you can imagine yourself singing in another place or time or age; or whether it's a song that requires you to take another's perspective. Doing this is a kind of song-perspective triage, as you should be able to sort all songs into one of the three following categories:

1. **Identification:** This is often the easiest kind of song to sing, as you need to do nothing other than be yourself in the present singing the lyric honestly, such as singing a love song to a loved one, or a lyric like "We Shall Overcome" from your own current perspective.
2. **Visualization:** In this technique you are still yourself, but you're imagining you're in a different place or time. You are at a loved one's funeral or deathbed, or transported back in time to Christmas morning as a child.
3. **Characterization:** This involves mentally stepping into another's skin, trying on someone else's perspective. Unlike acting, you do not need to take on this person's physical characteristics, wardrobe, speech patterns, and such. Your only task is to inhabit that person's perspective.

Let's take these approaches one at a time.

---

1 Caveat: There are ways for you to deliver a lyric you don't believe by presenting it in an extreme manner. For instance, an overly bombastic or sarcastic treatment of a song musically can undermine a lyric's message and in fact deliver the opposite. However, everyone in a group has to be in agreement as to this direction, as you can't have half of a group singing a song earnestly and another half singing it bitterly and ironically.

IDENTIFICATION

Singing is a way of releasing an emotion
that you sometimes can't portray when you're acting.
And music moves your soul, so music is the source of
the most intense emotions you can feel.
—AMANDA SEYFRIED

Some songs are in the first person, with frequent use of the word "I." These songs are often easy to sing because the point of view of the singer is clear. Others are in the third person ("he did this, she saw this") or, rarely, the second person ("you . . .").[1] Whichever the case may be, you need to decide two things:

• Who are you when singing the song?
• How do you feel about the events you're singing about?

If the answer is "I'm myself" and "the lyric represents the way I feel about the subject matter from my own experience," then you have the easiest kind of song to sing: one that you can personally deliver as yourself. You can step on stage and "live the song," delivering each word honestly as yourself.

As established earlier, people need to sing truthfully. Lyrics contain truth, but when they aren't being sung by the person who wrote them, they will fall flat unless the other people who sing them understand and accept this truth, which allows them to sing it honestly and powerfully as their own. Once someone other than the songwriter takes on this task and has developed an understanding of the meaning, that person becomes the "I" in a first-person song.

---

1 Note that a song isn't in the second person simply because it uses the word "you." It has to avoid "I" and, like a "choose your own adventure" book, tell you what is happening at each juncture—"you" do this, "you" do that. Sondheim's "Being Alive" is in the second person, as are Billy Joel's "Captain Jack," the Beatles' "For No One," Elvis's "Hound Dog," ABBA's "Dancing Queen," the Beastie Boys' "Fight for Your Right," and the Talking Heads' "Once in a Lifetime" ("You may find yourself living in a shotgun shack").

Many songs are open to different interpretations or easily sung about different people; that's what makes them universally felt and loved. For instance, the Beach Boys classic "God Only Knows" is a timeless song about one person's heartfelt appreciation for another. It can be sung by a man or woman, boy or girl, to a love interest, to a parent, to a friend. When singing this song, it doesn't matter who initially inspired Brian Wilson; you can fill the lyrics with your own feelings about your own special person. And so it goes for many of the greatest songs of all time: the universal becomes the specific as you fill the lyric with your own people, your own memories, your own details. The audience need never know who you are singing to, or why, if you don't want to tell them. Sing the song, and if it's real for you, it's real.

This point is critical. You need to find something in your life that gives you an understanding of the lyric personally, and a correlated feeling. This can take many forms:

- For a song about loss, you don't have to have lost the same person. If you're young and singing about death, you may not have lost a parent, but you may have lost a pet, or known someone who died, and experienced the feelings surrounding the event.
- For a song about injustice, you can draw on your own feelings of injustice about an issue that affects you personally, triggering anger and indignation.
- You may be able to draw on an appropriate feeling from an unrelated event in your own life. Maybe you're singing a song about a historical event that you don't feel connected to, or a dysfunctional relationship that you've never experienced. Look for an experience that evokes the feeling you need, ideally close enough to the lyrics such that singing the song continues to reinforce and underline your emotions.

Note that not every single lyric needs to be in complete alignment with your own experience. For instance, Three Dog Night's "Joy to the World" has a refrain that is uplifting and timeless. However, the first verse about the bullfrog Jeremiah may not make any sense. If you can assign Jeremiah's personality traits to a friend you have, you're in good shape. Or, occasionally, you can overlook a lyric, if it's a matter of hyperbole that strengthens the overall song. If you're singing Lorde's "Royals," you're not immediately disqualified if you have in fact seen a diamond in the flesh. I'm pretty sure at this point she has not only seen a diamond in the flesh but has plenty of her own, and yet she sings it night after night on tour.

For any group that is approaching the processes in this book for the first time, it's best to begin with songs the singers can perform as themselves in the present, as these are the most immediate and require the least amount of imagery and extrapolation. Once you become good at recalling emotions and bringing to life songs that are close to who you are, you'll be ready to further stretch your imagination and ability to recall emotions.

Although this is the most straightforward perspective from which to sing a song, that does not mean it will always be easy, as a song's lyrics and mood will not always match the singer's immediate frame of mind. Even direct and believable songs still require you to step on stage and sing with intensity, clarity, presence. If you're in a different mood, if you're bored, if you're having second thoughts about the lyric, if you no longer love the person you imagine yourself singing about, you're likely not going to be convincing. We'll address how to overcome these hurdles later.

VISUALIZATION

Everything you can imagine is real.
—PABLO PICASSO

Not every song is here and now, at least your own immediate here and now. Some songs are reminiscences; others are dreams for the future. Some remind you of a past relationship; others are about what you'll say to your children when they're grown, while in reality they're still young. To sing this kind of song, you're going to need to exercise your imagination and make the lyrics immediate through visualization.

Visualizing the past is easier than the future because it's concrete, so let's start there. Imagine you want to sing a song about Christmas morning, jumping out of bed and running to a tree surrounded by presents. There are a few steps that can help make this vague memory more present, more real:

1. **Get specific:** Don't settle for a loose mélange of past holidays; choose a specific Christmas morning.
2. **Use artifacts:** Do you have any photos from that morning? Any of your old toys still in storage somewhere? Physical objects and images can be very effective in helping you recall memories you haven't considered in ages.
3. **Focus on details:** What color was the wrapping paper? What did the ornaments look like? The more you can make your surroundings real, the easier it will be to recall them later on stage.
4. **Use all your senses:** What did the pine tree smell like? What did your pajamas feel like against your skin? Was the air in the living room warm or cold first thing in the morning? Could you hear the crackle of a log in the fireplace?

Some people find that writing things down helps their memories flow. Others like calling a relative or friend who shares the same memory, as together they'll remind each other of various details, reminiscing back and forth.

Once you have the memory clearly fleshed out in your mind, the next step is to practice recalling it in various situations. Maybe you're waiting for a doctor's appointment or just about to fall asleep. Close your eyes and recall the memory. Let the details and senses come flooding back. Try this in various places at various times; exercise your memory the way you would a muscle, so that it goes from an odd, foreign experience to something you are able to do on command.

Once you are able to recall the memory on demand, it's time to try it while singing. In some ways this should be easier, as the song's lyrics and the overall musical treatment should help you focus and return to that Christmas morning. If you're not perfectly able to bring back the memory at all times, do not get upset about it. Unless the song's mood is one of fear and frustration, you'll only flood your brain with the wrong emotion. Relax, realize no one is perfect, and keep singing. You don't want to distract any of your fellow singers, and by getting right back on the bike and riding you may find yourself gently slipping back into the memory and mood.

Another thing that can block you is the music itself. You want to sing the right notes, but you don't want to be *thinking* about the right notes, or rhythms, or cutoffs, and so on. To focus on the technical aspects of music while singing is to make the music about the technical aspects of singing, and that's almost certainly going to result in a dry, emotionless performance. It is possible to occasionally slip into "music mode" for a particularly difficult rubato moment or cue from the director, but these moments should be few and far between, the glow of the rest of your performance's emotional warmth still filling the hall. The time to focus on the song's mechanics is early on in the rehearsal process, while you're still learning and memorizing the notes. You need to move past this stage before you perform, or else you'll be no more compelling than a dancer who stares at his feet.

Some lyrics are not memories but are instead visions of the future—your future. For these, you should repeat the steps above, this time creating rather than recalling:

1. Get specific: Where will you be when this moment takes place? What will you be wearing; what's the weather like?

2. Use artifacts: Is there anything you have now that you will still have then? Does the song take place in 30 years around the piano that you're playing right now? These concrete items help anchor the future as real.

3. Focus on details: For each of the lyrics in the song, flesh out details. If there's a book, what is the book? Does it have a leather cover? Is it sitting on your lap or on the table?

4. Use all your senses: What does the air smell like? Can you hear birds chirping or snow falling as the wind rustles the pine trees?

And so on. You may fill this world with incredible detail or prefer a few key points in focus with the rest remaining in loose brushstrokes. What matters is how this world appears to you, as it needs to be real, a place you can recall and inhabit as you sing the song. Know that each time you reenter this world it does not have to be exactly the same; like the movie *Groundhog Day* you can clarify and alter the details as you return time and again to the same moment, each time refining to create in yourself the exact emotion you want to portray.

If this sounds fun, that's because it is! Singing a song is no longer a march on stage, a series of songs where you stare at the director and hope you don't make a mistake. Most high school choral singers worry more about singing a wrong note than they do about conveying the emotion of a song, which is a failing of our educational system. Music is not math. There is not only one correct way to present a song on stage, not only one precise set of notes that makes for the perfect arrangement, one perfect choral tone, one exacting set of tuned chords. You should be singing a song to make the audience cry, laugh, clap along, and want to join choir next semester. That is how you do high school choral music right, and for that matter all music. How many people come up to you after a concert and tell you how great you made them feel, how much fun they could tell you were having? How many ask if they could audition for the group? That's what music is and has been and should be. Visualize that before you go on stage, and in time it will come true.

CHARACTER

*I feel like I'm able to relate to all races of people
because when you learn to tap into the raw emotion of a person,
that goes past color.*
—BIG SEAN

Some songs are incredibly compelling, thoroughly in alignment with your view of the world, and something you'd very much like to say, but outside your own personal experience. This doesn't preclude you from singing the song. If it did, most people would not be able to sing most songs believably. There's an old saying: "You can't really understand someone until you've walked a mile in their shoes." Obviously in all but the rarest circumstances this is impossible, but for our purposes you'll be doing the walking in your imagination, which is far easier and results in fewer blisters.

It's important to note that the focus here will be on understanding and inhabiting another's skin. You won't be going so far as to be acting like this person, but you will be drawing on important acting principles as you embody the character that is singing the song, then breathe life into the character by drawing on experiences from your own life. If you are a successful actor, by all means you should feel free to use all of your techniques and experience to deliver songs on stage. I do not want anyone to think I am against acting. Rather, I do not believe acting technique is necessary to be a great singer or performer, as has been evidenced throughout music history.

What you will be doing is not acting, but it might be considered halfway to acting. You're not going to become someone else, but you are going to imagine being someone else, which is a crucial step actors take down that path to creating character.

Unlike actors, you do not need to take on another person's physical manifestations, nor do you need to create a persona that will carry you through a two-hour movie or play. Your character is limited in most cases to a single moment or series of actions through a three-minute song, so your scope is contained and the number of considerations is much lower.

The questions you should ask regarding the character are the ones that are cogent to the song and take you out of yourself: Who is the person at the center of the song whose shoes you will wear? What are that person's cares and worries? What happens during the song and what role does the person play? And, most importantly, what does this person feel about it all? That last question, the one of feelings, is the key to unlocking it all. The act of empathy is what will place you in the individual's shoes, and it is what will place the audience in those same shoes if you sing the song with conviction. Once you've mastered singing songs from your own perspective, both in the present and in various situations, you are ready to expand your horizons, stretching further and further from yourself as you sing songs by characters who are less and less like you.

Every decision about a character does not need to be fully agreed upon by everyone in the group, so long as the varying interpretations are not at odds. In fact, in some cases not every singer needs to be the same person. When singing the Christmas classic "Do You Hear What I Hear," one member of the choir may like to think of himself as a shepherd, another as an angel. For the purposes of the song and performance, it doesn't really matter. What matters is for each person singing to have a clear sense of identity that is emotionally grounded in the lyric.

It's also not always the case that a song requires a character, if it can be sung by any individual. "We Wish You a Merry Christmas" can be expressed in character, or simply as oneself, wishing the audience a merry Christmas. No need to make things more complicated. If you recently ran into an old lover and you talked about old times over a beer, you might be able to sing Paul Simon's "Still Crazy After All These Years" entirely or at least largely as yourself. If not, perhaps you can imagine this happening in the future. If that's not likely for whatever reason, you can inhabit the character at the center of the song, which may or may not be Paul Simon himself. In time you will experience a fluidity between your own and others' perspectives, the common link at all times being the universal feelings we all feel and the empathy necessary for you to inhabit another person's skin. This will allow you to express the song in such a way as to make the audience join you within that skin.

SUBSTITUTION

I reject your reality and substitute my own.
—ADAM SAVAGE

Perhaps you're singing a song with a woman's name in the title, and you don't know anyone by that name? Think of someone else when singing the name. This can also work with locations, seasons, etc. Your job as singer is to channel honest emotion into each lyric, making the songwriter's words your own, and sometimes the best way to do this is by substituting your own specifics.

It may not be as simple as one-for-one transfer, as may be the case when singing about a person. Some songs can get rather specific, in which case you may find yourself taking attributes from a few different people in your life to create a composite that best fills the person described in the lyrics. There's nothing false about this, as every word is true, it's just that they're true about different people for you. Sometimes the opposite is true, as in the case of "You're So Vain," by Carly Simon. Many people who have sung this song have assumed it to be about one person, but in fact each verse is about a different person in the songwriter's young life. Lyrics can be complicated this way, not reflecting one exact moment or person, but rather a pastiche of events, thoughts, people, and feelings. You may approach your interpretation of the song in the same way.

You may also find substitution valuable when singing religious songs. Many schools have a choral concert in December that celebrates multiple faiths. And many professional groups will find December their busiest month, as it is a time that is traditionally associated with vocal music (caroling, holiday concerts, etc.). As a result, you may find yourself singing a song or even an entire concert that does not reflect your own faith. When this happens, you will likely find it helpful to substitute your own feelings, beliefs, faith, spirituality. And if you don't have faith? Then sing about something you do believe in. Unless you're going to refuse to perform for a moral or ethical reason, when you step on the stage you have a responsibility to create something real, honest, impactful. Find your truth within the lyric and make the song true for you.

Once you have access to the appropriate emotion(s), the next step is to figure out, is your song a moment, or does it have a plot?

PLOT

Plot is no more than footprints left in the snow
after your characters have run by on their way to incredible destinations.
—RAY BRADBURY

By this point, several things should be clear: who you are while singing, where you are, and who is there with you. The stage is set. The next step is to understand how those elements change over the course of the song as it moves through time, a sequence of events, a plot.

The key points when considering the plot are:

- How does the song start? What is the state of everything at the beginning?
- What changes during the course of the song? What is the state at the end?
- How do I as the singer feel each step of the way?

Your task remains the same as we've discussed; the one additional variable is that your emotion will shift appropriately through the song. Through understanding and empathizing with the characters and situations in your plot, fueled by your own feelings, substituting as needed, you will be injecting your performance with emotion that is both real and appropriate. This is similar to an actor's process, but unlike an actor you are never anyone other than yourself on stage: no character name is needed, no costume, no other setting, props, or other actors to interact with. You're yourself, with a story to tell and memories or fantasies to draw upon, a reminiscence or dream that brings to light your own feelings and beliefs in a framework written by someone else, but nonetheless true.

Note that occasionally a song will have a shifting narrator accompany the plot, or the nature of the plot will come from multiple people singing about the same moment from their perspective. In musical theater, each character is generally portrayed by a different singer (such as in West Side Story's "Quintet"), but in a concert you will likely remain in the driver's seat throughout, even when the perspective or point of view changes. As above, create a pastiche to bring meaning to each of the perspectives. So long as each moment is real, the overall performance will work.

MOMENT

Be happy in the moment; that's enough.
Each moment is all we need, not more.
—MOTHER TERESA

Not every song is a story; not every lyric has a progression and journey. Some focus on a place, a time, a memory, a moment. Lyrics of this nature often do not require more than one emotion, but that emotion may be multifaceted, layered, and nuanced. Your group's understanding and embrace of this moment needs to be complete, lest your performance feel flat or two-dimensional. In other words, if you're playing just one emotional note over and over again throughout the song, it needs to be a good one.

You might occasionally think that a song is a moment but find upon looking more closely that what at first feels static and perhaps poetic in fact reflects a progression in the singer's perspective. One example would be "Both Sides Now," by Joni Mitchell. It appears to be a simple revelation that perspective and time shift one's understanding, but upon closer examination the song's statement about the variance of clouds becomes a statement about love and finally about life. This moving perspective and greater revelation as the song progresses is indeed a plot, if a cerebral one, and should be treated as a song that changes, rather than remaining the same throughout.

Either way, each song you perform should be a moment of truth. If the song exemplifies a feeling or memory to which your group cannot relate, it is either time to dig deep and find meaning you can relate to or time to find a new song. (There's always a third option: to go make some memories that adhere to the songwriter's vision and the story's journey. Of course, in some cases that's a very bad idea.) You do not have to hew exactly to every line and detail, but you and your group must be able to make this moment real, believable, emotionally powerful, poignant. You must justify your singing of the song.

Children are cute; children can sing anything and we as adults understand that the real message is "Watch us sing; enjoy our youth." Occasionally there can be another layer of meaning, but it's rarely the case, and we don't expect it. Once we grow older, just as our essays become more focused, our public speeches are expected to be interesting, and our conversations with people cannot repeatedly disregard the subject at hand for whatever happens to be on your mind at the moment. Similarly, when we sing, we must say something of value. To sing a song simply because you like it, unless the theme of the song supports that notion (like a happy song about singing), is ultimately an act of selfishness.

I recall one weekend afternoon as a pre-teen when my sister dragged me into some play she and her friends were putting on. It wasn't scripted, it had no point, and it continued to change to their whims. She invited my mom down to the basement to watch, where after three acts of nonsense our invited audience declared, "You should know better," and went back upstairs. It struck me as a little harsh at the time, but I came to realize that she expected us at that age to have created something rather than just play in front of her while demanding her attention. Performing by its very nature demands audience attention, and that attention is a responsibility, a contract we must fulfill. It cannot just be us doing what we want. Music is a gift; we must give something.

It is possible through arrangement and performance choices to take a song and make it mean something different, altering a moment to reflect something that's more meaningful to your group. That's absolutely fine. "Make it your own" is often spoken in the walls of conservatories and record labels, and this is what it means. Don't just change a song for the purpose of making it different; change it for the purpose of making it meaningful to you and expressive of your own experience and perspective.

TRIGGERS

I'm an actor who believes we all have triggers to any stage of emotion.
It's not always easy to find, but it's still there.
—Hugh Jackman

In psychology and acting, an emotional trigger is a situation, comment, action, or memory that causes one to snap into a pronounced emotional state. We all have them, and whereas they can be problematic when arising in social situations, they can be useful for our musical purposes. Before going any further it is important that you recognize that the act of digging around for emotional triggers may call up some difficult memories that can take time and care to process. Make sure you have someone you can turn to if you need support, and do not hesitate to look into therapy if the feelings become overwhelming. We are complex beings and should not feel any shame when turning to an expert who can help us understand our most powerful emotions.

At their most effective, emotional triggers give us immediate access to specific feelings through words, actions, memories, or mental images. As you uncover them, you can think of each trigger as a specific tool or key you can use to unlock a mood. Some memories are immediately present; others require some digging. Some memories are emotionally overwhelming, others gentle. Some are a single, pure, clear emotion, others nuanced. We have as many emotional triggers as we have memories. The trick is to choose the right one for the right situation.

Once you have decided upon an appropriate, strong, and ideally somewhat easily triggered emotional memory, the next step is to practice accessing it. Choose different times of day, different locations, different baseline moods. See if you are able to return the memory and feeling to the front of your mind. Sometimes senses can be very helpful during this process, as you recall the sights, sounds, smells, sensations you felt as the emotion was present, although you will not be able to pull out a series of photographs or an aromatherapy bottle on stage in the middle of a song. You can initially use these items to make the emotions present, then practice recalling the moments without them.

If you're not an actor, this is not a process that will feel comfortable or second nature to you. We learn to suppress emotions but not to recall them on demand. Like a muscle that has not been used, this technique will require some time to become fluent. That is normal. Don't expect perfection when you first start, any more than a person just learning to sing should expect every note to be in perfect tune. Like building muscle tissue, with repetition and practice it will become easier and more automatic. Practice makes perfect.

The biggest challenge is to dial up the appropriate amount of the emotion you seek. Some memories, especially those that are recent or involve loss of a loved one, can quickly overwhelm us. Others are delicate and distant, requiring us to focus and delve deeper to bring up the mood. Consider the gas pedal on your car: sometimes you're driving uphill, sometimes downhill, and the latter requires less effort from your engine. Sometimes you need no effort, only the steering wheel, as gravity will pull you along as quickly as you need to go. Sometimes you even need to apply the brake. So it is with emotions as well. You're in the driver's seat with the tools you need to get where you want to go. With experience you'll become a good driver.

Techniques

EMOTIONAL-TECHNICAL CONNECTION

To the person who uses music as a medium for the expression of ideas,
feelings, images, or what have you, anything which facilitates
this expression is properly his instrument.
—BILL EVANS

All of this focus on emotions may have you concerned, especially if you're a director. What about the tuning? What about the blend? The fact is that good emotional singing almost always results in good technical singing. Even if you're not sure why, you likely have realized that when the technical elements of a performance get better, the emotional performance and unity of the group similarly improves. The converse is also true: when the emotion is properly dialed in, a group's musical technique also improves.

The reason for this connection in both directions is synergy. If your singers are all singing with a smile, their vowels are more aligned, their overtones alike. To look at it from the other direction, if they're all singing appropriately bright vowels with raised eyebrows and good resonance, they're all likely moving the same facial muscles that are involved in smiling and, as mentioned earlier, this increases happiness. The same goes for furrowed brows, contracted cheek muscles, and narrowed eyes and lips in pursuit of a dark tone or an angry countenance. Your facial expressions affect the resonance chambers in your mouth, sinuses, and throat.

Every technical improvement you're making to your group's sound is benefiting the overall emotion of the song. Think of it this way: your mood colors your sound, and your sound colors your mood. Sometimes it's a small move in the right direction; sometimes it's a breakthrough. Of course, flawless technique doesn't alone equal flawless emotional understanding and expression, any more than only understanding a song emotionally will result in precise choral singing. Time must be spent in rehearsal on both aspects of music to create a superlative performance.

Now is a good time to issue a warning: be sure to avoid "indicating" otherwise known as bad acting. It does not work to simply move your body and face around in a grotesque pantomime as if you're actually feeling an emotion. There's a not-so-fine line between a fist that clenches as a feeling is being conjured and a flailing fist as a singer stomps around the stage. Just as too much makeup is garish and off-putting, too many gestures indicating an emotion are off-putting and do not effectively substitute for the real thing. Less is more and, as you cannot conjure emotion purely through physical attributes, accentuating those motions does not lead to greater emotion.

If you're the group's music director, you likely suffer from what I call "music director's disease": the impulse to edit, to analyze your performance as it transpires, trying to remember every error so that you'll be able to address it all Monday morning. When you focus on technique, you're not emoting. Your face likely goes blank. How can you combat this horrible, lifelong affliction? You have to let go. Turn off the editor, focus on the lyric, and do everything you tell your singers to do. Sure, the occasional error will snap you out of your blissful emoting, but just log it and go back to being a singer. If you're not able to let go, record your performances (audio or video) so you can "sing now, analyze later."

The key is to prepare the emotion using emotional techniques and the musical elements using musical techniques; then on stage your singers should be able to represent both without focusing on either. You cannot feel sad by thinking, "Feel sad! Feel sad!" and you cannot make great music simply by focusing on tuning. The work should be done in rehearsal, so that in performance the focus can be on connecting with the audience and reveling in the music itself while creating it. Preparation is key, as singers can more easily get "lost" in a performance when it's good.

Some use the expression "riding the wave," like a surfer who catches the wave at just the right time and feels like she's flying, effortlessly able to enjoy the moment without a care. If a singer is worried about tuning, entrances, dynamics, and other technical elements of a performance, she's distracted from making an emotional connection to the song. And if she's trying too hard to be emotional, neither the emotion nor the technical aspects of the song will align. Much like Aesop's fable about the wind and the sun at the beginning of this book, you cannot force great musical performance. When properly approached, like the rays of the sun, it will shine from within.

THRESHOLDS

Technique should be taught, not as an end in itself,
but as something related to individual expression, as a means
toward an end. One cannot separate technique from expression.
There is only expression.
—KIMON NICOLAIDES

No two people have the same musical taste, and no two people have the same musical ears. We all have a different understanding of what constitutes beauty, and the concepts of "in tune" and "in the groove" can vary from performer to performer, style to style, mood to mood. There is no one perfect standard by which music can be judged, or by which you can be sure your music will be accepted by others. The best you can do is to make your music carry the emotions you want it to, and to be as precise as you can manage, knowing that no music is in perfect tune, and in fact our Western tuning system has been compromised since the time of J. S. Bach.[1]

For emotions to register in each audience member, the performer's technique needs to clear a certain threshold. The tuning, rhythm, and other technical elements can't be problematically distracting, or else the listener's focus will be thrown, the aesthetics tainted. We can all tolerate a rather high amount of musical imprecision when we hear a group of kindergarteners sing a Christmas carol, but as the performers get older we expect more, just as expectations change based on the setting (karaoke bar or concert hall), ticket price, and a variety of different factors.

I recall a very powerful performance by the Brigham Young University Vocal Point, a ballad dedicated on *The Sing-Off* to the

---

1   If you are not familiar with the harmonic series and the ways in which our scale is intentionally slightly out of tune, you can find explanations online and in books. Suffice it to say that we are completely acclimated to music that is out of tune, so our musical ears, as perfect as we may think they are, have limitations and culturally reinforced imperfections. And yes, a cappella groups can hypothetically sing in better tune than most instruments, but of course we are imperfect by our very nature and can at best approach perfection, never attain it.

father of one of the members, who had died a few nights before. The dress rehearsal was near flawless, but as the cameras rolled, emotion got the better of the group and the performance suffered technically. Knowing the situation, that emotion just made the performance that much more impactful, and the judges applauded the singers' bravery during such a difficult time.

I mention this as an example of emotion overwhelming technique without distancing the audience, but these times are few and far between. The audience's trust should not be taken advantage of, nor should this kind of situation be intentionally returned to with any frequency.

Don't think that the techniques in this book are a "get out of jail free" card, allowing you to fudge good technique and substitute raw emotion. There are times when emotion gets the better of us, but it cannot be an excuse, just as focusing on technique is no excuse for not having an emotionally centered performance.

ACTOR'S TECHNIQUES

We are what we pretend to be,
so we must be careful about what we pretend to be.
—Kurt Vonnegut

There are a few techniques that actors use to better understand emotion that you may find useful. Those studying musical theater or opera likely get some experience with these techniques, which can be valuable to all singers, regardless of style:

Workbook: Some actors keep a notebook of emotions, experiences, images, and triggers, which they continuously expand and refer back to as necessary. Others will write out a complete "character study" for every character they play, creating a complex backstory filled with a number of details that may never surface yet help create a fully nuanced, three-dimensional performance.

Motivation: As a singer, you might imagine obstacles to help motivate your performance, such as a person you need to convince, a crowd you're preaching to, an audience listening to a story you're telling that if successful will change the course of history. These techniques may be too much for some, but if you have an active imagination (like James Thurber's Walter Mitty) and like fantasy or role playing, you may find this process of finding your motivation productive and fun.

Exploration: In rehearsal, an actor spends time exploring emotions not necessarily connected to any specific role. She might talk with fellow actors, friends, or coaches about past experiences and feelings, gaining access in order to recall them later when needed. Actors also will explore and critique each other's performances in workshops, noting which portrayals feel honest and which false. This hasn't been and isn't an element of music study, but it likely should be, as we are as responsible for the emotional experience of our audience as actors are.

FIRST TIME

Do not say, "It is morning," and dismiss it with a name of yesterday.
See it for the first time as a newborn child that has no name.
—Rabindranath Tagore

One of the key principles stage actors are told is that they need to make every performance feel like it's happening for the first time. Every line, every reaction, every nuance needs to flow from the moment that happened just before it. This is challenging but central to a great performance. Movies and television can be edited together to craft the right moments from a collection of takes and attempts, but stage acting requires the ability to experience things for the first time over and over again.

Once your singers are accessing their emotions in a controlled way, tackling songs that touch on more challenging emotions and memories, the next step will be to introduce songs that tell a story, take the singer and listener on a journey. These songs are built on lyrics that happen through time (such as Harry Chapin's "Cat's in the Cradle" or Meatloaf's "Paradise by the Dashboard Light") as opposed to those that capture a single moment (such as "Oh, What a Beautiful Morning").

Story songs unfold through time, with plot twists and character development, requiring one or more change in mood over the course of the song. Obviously, you as a singer know what's coming, and perhaps the audience does as well, if they're familiar with the song; and yet the poignancy in the song comes from the emotional shifts, which sometimes require surprise. David Bowie's "Space Oddity" is far less powerful if the song carries the same emotion from the beginning to the end. It should bring forth feelings of anticipation, wonder, and eventually sadness, all at the right times. And for this to happen as powerfully as a stage actor delivers lines, it should feel as if the story is unfolding in real time, the song's final revelation coming as a surprise, a shock, a feeling of loss akin to the one you felt when you first listened to the lyrics.

PURPOSE

Efforts and courage are not enough without purpose and direction.
—JOHN F. KENNEDY

Opera choristers are usually vibrant performers, marrying technique with emotional expression effortlessly. For some, acting training may contribute to this effect, but when the entire chorus creates a believable world on stage, a more likely reason is that they have a clear purpose.

The singers know why they're on stage, what they are meant to do. They have a role, a piece of the story to further, a moment to create. This may sound obvious, but many choirs don't perform with the same intensity, because they don't have or know their purpose.

This isn't because there's less of a "reason" for choral music, or collegiate a cappella, or any of the other forms of vocal harmony. We all chose to join our groups and return each week to rehearsals for myriad reasons. We choose specific songs for a reason, we step on stage with a purpose, and yet too often the lights hit faces, the starting pitch is played, and it all becomes about singing the right notes.

I frequently ask groups, "Why are you singing this song?" and get no reply. Hoping to tap into their love of music and drive to perform, I ask, "Why do you sing? Why are you in this choir?" and more often than not am met with wide-eyed silence, as if they'd never really considered it. This isn't a trick question. I want to know their reasons, their motivations, their purpose to help rekindle their flame, or, if it's bright, to help them hold it high where all can see. Too often they have forgotten or buried their desires, love of music, and raison d'être, perhaps because they think it's not appropriate to think about these things on stage. Nothing could be more appropriate! If you're a singer but don't know why you're on stage or what you're doing there, you can't expect an audience to care. Know yourself, know your music, know your purpose.

If it helps, think of your performance as a step in a journey, a task in a game that must be undertaken at the highest level in order to complete your mission. And what is that task? Each song is different, and yet the overarching goal is the same: to bring joy, understanding, and empathy into people's lives. To help make sense of our existence. To inspire others to join us and bring singing back into their lives at a time when fewer people make music than ever before—thanks to an educational system that rates music as second or third class, a society that has recorded music at our fingertips, and a popular culture that frequently publicly mocks imperfect singers, such as *American Idol.*

It used to be the case that everybody sang: around the campfire, around the spinet, around the barbershop. Church services and community gatherings often included song. We as a culture have lost that. Now that we can listen to music everywhere we go, we no longer "need" to generate it ourselves . . . and yet we're all songbirds, crickets, whales. We're hard-wired to sing, which is why so many sing in the shower, sing in the car, get drunk to overcome their inhibition to sing karaoke . . . and yet it isn't enough. We need to sing to each other and with each other regularly. When you sing, remember this. Realize there is likely someone in the audience at every show who wants to sing. Inspire them to join you. You will be making the world a better place, one concert, one person at a time.

SINGING BY MEMORY

The best memorizers in all the world—who almost all hail
from Europe—can memorize a (shuffled) pack of cards
in less than a minute.
—Joshua Foer

It likely goes without saying, but let's make sure the point is clear: it is nearly impossible for a choir to perform at its peak both musically and emotionally if their heads are buried in sheet music. Certainly there will be times when sheet music is needed, such as a last-minute performance opportunity, or casual caroling for the community, but they should be the exception, not the rule.

Obviously, it takes additional time to memorize a piece of music, and yet all but the most complex are performed every day of the year all around the globe by memory. How can you get your group singing from memory more often?

- Provide your singers with recordings and/or videos of good performances of the piece, so they can hear how it goes.
- In addition to sheet music, provide learning recordings if possible, i.e., one voice on a particular singer's part in one ear, the rest of the parts in the other. You can also use a MIDI or music notation file to play the parts, or just sit at the piano and record parts.
- Have your singers use a recording device (a smartphone should work) to record key sections of the rehearsal as well as the last time through each song so they can listen, practice, and memorize on their own.
- Before each rehearsal, singers should review the last recording so they can pick up right where they left off.

The integration of frequent recordings and self-review into your rehearsal process can dramatically increase the speed of note learning and memorization.

If you want your group to be truly transformative singers, if you want them to connect with the audience, if you want to create memories that will not soon be forgotten, then your singers will have to put down the sheet music before they step on stage.

FOREIGN LANGUAGES

To have another language is to possess a second soul.
—CHARLEMAGNE

To sing in another language requires just as much text analysis and emotional focus as you bring to bear on songs in your native language and the language of your audience. In fact, you may need to bring heightened emotion to bear, as you can't rely on people understanding and being moved by the lyric.

It helps for you to learn and remember some of the foreign words, if not all of them. The title, lyrics that are repeated, key words like "love"—all can be very valuable to keep you focused on the story, the emotion. Hopefully there are some cognates, some similar words, some phrases you can remember.

Other languages can be very beautiful: the sound of their words, the way they turn a phrase, pair together images, create their own idioms. Find something to love about these words so you can sing them with true appreciation.

VOCAL TONE

The human voice is the most beautiful instrument of all,
but it is the most difficult to play.
—RICHARD STRAUSS

A group experiencing and expressing the same emotion will be matching their vowels, bright or dark, happy or sad, and yet some choral directors fear that unbridled emotional singing will ruin traditionally accepted proper vocal tone. Nothing could be farther from the truth.

In a quest for tall, resonant vowels, and in hopes of avoiding spread, bright vowels, proponents of "inner smiling" urge singers not to smile when they sing. This is not necessary, as choral directors can have the best of both worlds. By raising the upper lip, a singer can still smile without overly widening and compromising tone. In more technical terms, the zygomaticus major and minor are linked to emotion. To freeze these muscles and not allow a full range of motion has the negative effect of stifling natural emotional reactions.

If all of this technical jargon made little sense, suffice it to say: smiling while you sing does not result in improper vocal tone and technique. On the contrary, to not smile when you're singing a song about smiling is ridiculous. Joy should be expressed as we express joy, and the universally understood physical attributes that the human species has developed to express emotion should not be suppressed. If truth is beauty and beauty truth, you should not avoid the simplest truth of all: smiling and singing when you are happy.

SYLLABLES

Yabba, dabba, doo!
—FRED FLINTSTONE

Vocal harmony is increasingly rife with a variety of sounds and syllables that are neither lyrics nor simple open vowels. Contemporary a cappella in particular is pushing the boundaries of vocal timbre with a great deal of instrumental imitation (most notably and frequently vocal percussion) and a wide range of non-lyrical syllables intended to emphasize tone color and create a range of sounds for a vocal group that allows a depth and variety of sound.

The result is often an ensemble in which one person is singing the melody and a dozen other people are singing nothing at all resembling words. And yet they're on stage singing, and the performance relies on their expression, their emotion. You may not be speaking words, but you're always saying something.

We don't question this when it's a gospel choir singing "hmm" under a powerful soloist, or a choir on a full-throated "ah." Is there a difference between these syllables and the newer ones now in use? No. None. A song is a song, a mood is a mood, and a vocal group remains able to sing every sound with meaning, whatever the sound may be.

Having trouble with this? The first step is to focus on the lead vocal lyrics, as they're the focal point for the audience. Another option is to imagine yourself an instrumentalist, which is especially fitting if your vocal line is imitative. Guitars? Be Keith Richards or Jimi Hendrix. Trumpets? Maybe you're the Tower of Power horns, or Herb Alpert. Go with whatever inspires you, whatever works.

There are rare instances in which the background syllable distracts from or works against your interpretation of the song. Sometimes an arranger will pick a sound that is difficult to sing, or maybe you're singing a song in a different language, country or culture and what was a nonsense syllable just took on a new meaning.[1] By all means, change the syllable to something else that works and is easier to sing, less distracting, and doesn't carry an unintended meaning.

Sometimes the lyric itself has meaningless syllables, from the "fa la la" in "Deck the Hall" and many madrigals, to the "na na na" in "Kiss Him Goodbye." The mood is clear and easily gleaned from the surrounding lyrics if ever in doubt. If you need further inspiration, scat singing is full of style, personality, and nuance, even though the syllables are themselves non-linguistic. A sax and trumpet can express emotion, as can a person imitating their sound, and so can a singer who is scatting. Louis Armstrong, Ella Fitzgerald, and many others brought great artistry to their scat singing, all the while filling each sound with feeling.

---

1   The business world is rife with stories of misnamed products, resulting from a positive word or image in one language becoming negative in another. The Internet is full of examples, such as the name of an extremely popular soda in Ghana. Even though it means "very good cola," Pee Cola is unlikely to catch on in the U.S.

REPETITION

What so tedious as a twice-told tale?
—HOMER

Repetition exists in music for a reason: we need something to hold on to, something familiar, a refrain. Through-composed music can be beautiful, but it rarely wins enough fans to qualify as popular music. Without repetition, an audience may lose interest; but excessive repetition will bore them, too.

Songs are written for the audience, so the composer sets the frequency of the chorus, the hook, the motifs woven into the song with them in mind. Most members of any given audience are likely hearing your performance of a song for the first time, making repetition all the more essential. Perhaps you and your fellow singers have been singing a song over and over again in rehearsal and would prefer less repetition? Just remember that the performance is for them, not for you, and recall your first time singing through the song when it was all fresh, new, and exciting.

That said, there are times when a vocal harmony song should be distilled and reduced in length. My experience tells me that vocal harmony is a heightened experience for the audience that transmits emotional energy with a special intensity. As a result, a five-minute radio track is better at three or three and a half minutes in a cappella performance. People lose focus when listening to the radio, drift off, come back when the chorus returns, drift off again . . . and you don't want that. Trim the introduction, perhaps the third verse, perhaps the fourth iteration of the chorus at the end. Less is more for your audience, and for your fellow singers.

Nonetheless, even with reductions you may be singing the same chorus several times in an arrangement, or perhaps you have a single repeated phrase, a two- or four- measure bass line, a vocal part that does the same thing over and over and over again, which is important for the overall aesthetic but dull for you. What can you do? Start by remembering that live vocal music does not have to be like a song on the radio, which is to say it should have dynamics. Modern popular music is so thoroughly compressed (so you have a consistent wall of sound while driving, dancing, etc.) that people singing popular music often forget that dynamic variation is one of the four dimensions of music, and critical to a powerful performance. Slowly build through a verse, give a two-measure phrase a rise and fall, and generally breathe life into passages with the same notes and rhythms.

If this isn't enough, consider adding a small amount of variation to mix it up—a little rhythmic beat at the end of a line, a vowel change each time you return to the verse, moving chords up an inversion later in the song. Make things different, not necessarily because the music itself demands it, but because you need it and you're the music. A great arrangement that bores you to tears isn't a great arrangement. We're not player pianos, we're not programmed synthesizer loops. Singers must be engaged. It's an essential element of vocal arranging.

Even with a fantastic song, an engaging arrangement, and ideal circumstances, you'll still sometimes find yourself sidetracked, losing focus, and slipping into "autopilot." What is autopilot?

AUTOPILOT

As an actor, being on autopilot is the worst thing possible.
—Matthew Perry

utopilot is an expression for any time a singer loses focus and disengages while singing. Ideally, it would never happen, but when a member feels he isn't important with so many others around singing the same part, he may "zone out" during a performance, producing a blank stare, a lower intensity level, and no emotional connection to the music.

If you find yourself slipping into autopilot, throw yourself back into the lyrics, the meaning, your trigger emotions. Look in the eyes of the other singers in your group or your director, find someone who is fully engaged, and connect with that person, as he or she can slingshot you back into being "in the moment." Relax for a moment between songs, then focus during songs.

If you see a fellow singer whose eyes are glazed over, look right into his eyes and try to engage him. If you're standing beside him you can nudge him, move with him, try to pull him into your "sphere of influence" and snap him out of his daydream. You'll know when he's back—you can see it in his eyes, hear it in his voice. And if you happen to see a fellow singer staring right at you, don't take it personally. We all lose focus from time to time. Get back in the game and return the favor sometime.

If you find your group drifting into autopilot frequently during a specific song, it could be the choice of song or arrangement. Do they care about the song's topic and message? Do they like the song? Is the arrangement too repetitive, too easy, too boring? Make sure you choose engaging repertoire that marries well with your group's beliefs and experiences, and aim for the proper level of difficulty and repetition in each arrangement. A few changes to an existing arrangement that they find dull (adding a key change, adding rhythmic or melodic complexity to an ostinato background line) can make a noticeable difference.

THE SPACES BETWEEN

Never miss a good chance to shut up.
—WILL ROGERS

A song doesn't begin when you start singing; it begins at the first breath before the first note, just as your performance begins when you first set foot on stage. The rests in the music are sonic releases but not necessarily emotional ones, and you can't let go and relax just because you perceive that you're not doing anything, because in fact you are.

Every moment in a song, composition, and arrangement exists for a reason, and the overall success of each moment requires continued focus, attention, emotional intensity. Don't stop, don't slack off, don't let your fellow singers down. "Sing" the rests, emote through the silences. Just as a great actor must listen to others dialogue intently, so too must you remain focused, connected, and "in the moment" throughout your performance of every song. You are taking your audience on a journey, and you want them to feel comfortable throughout, as though they're in the hands of a great movie director presenting them with one carefully chosen scene after another. Vocal bands can inject a cavalier, casual attitude between songs, but to do so while holding the audience's focus in a professional way is deceptively simple. Larger groups, especially choirs, just can't relax with the same ease, as the loose shuffling of a hundred bodies on risers is distracting behind even the most charismatic emcee.

One of the most identifiable elements of an amateur group is the way they handle the end of each song. A quickly clipped last note and nervous shuffling to your next position tells the audience you don't believe in your music or your performance. Do not release the end of a song until the last note has rung out through the audience and the moment dissipates. Hold still, revel in and savor the last chord and the lingering silence that follows. Then stay in place and accept the audience's applause graciously. Only then should you move to the next position. Just as an Olympic gymnast must "stick the landing" to demonstrate complete control, so must your group indicate to the audience an effortless control over each moment on stage.

Considerations

IMPORTANCE OF THE INDIVIDUAL

Individual commitment to a group effort—that is what makes
a team work, a company work, a civilization work.
—VINCE LOMBARDI

Whereas harmony singing is very much about the sum of the parts being greater than any one voice, emotional singing starts and ends with the individual.

Singing, by its very definition, is a communal act. As with speaking, sound is being created for someone else to hear. It's an act of sharing, of extroversion.

Emotions, on the other hand, are something that most contemporary cultures deem personal, not communal. We express openly as infants, and as we grow older and are socialized, we learn to divert, repress, and quiet our emotions when in public so as not to make other people uncomfortable or disrupt whatever work is being done. Overt expressions of sadness, anger, even joy are rarely seen in the grocery store, in the office, on the street. People generally share their emotions in more intimate settings with those close to them.

For this reason, it is an act of bravery to fight against one's learned instincts and express in public. It takes determined individuals to step outside their usual modes of interaction and comfort so they can feel publicly, and this emotion needs to be harnessed, channeled into the music.

To cultivate courage in your group, you as the director, aided by like-minded members of the group, must take the first steps, leading by example. This isn't about creating awkward emotional moments out of context, but rather revealing meaningful insights and connections during discussions, showing how much more powerful a vocal performance can be when honest, and reinforcing the points made throughout this book alongside the more traditional musical techniques that are mentioned in every rehearsal. If you want your group to discover greater emotional openness and power in performance, know that it won't "just happen." People need to make the change happen, one person at a time.

REHEARSAL CONSISTENCY

We will meet; and there we may rehearse
most obscenely and courageously.
—SHAKESPEARE

Perhaps the single most important principle for you to remember in rehearsal is this: the way you rehearse is the way you perform. Attempting to add emotion at the last moment before a performance, or having a discussion early in the process and then not referencing it until dress rehearsal, sends the message to your singers that it doesn't really matter. If the key to excellence is focused repetition, then you will need to make sure emotion is part of that repetition.

To do this, you don't need to have repeated lengthy discussions; just reference your previous discussion, reminding people of the few key words you distilled. One way to keep emotion present in everyone's mind is to reference the emotional reason behind musical choices where appropriate. A *subito piano* might emphasize a moment of surprise in the lyrics, while a gradual build in dynamics supports a build in emotional intensity. Any director's choices should be grounded in the emotion throughout, so this shouldn't be a challenge. When musical directions have a purpose, singers remember and execute them with more conviction. Then, in performance, each crescendo and staccato will remind singers of their emotional journey throughout the song.

Another benefit of referencing emotion is that it will become just another element of your group's culture, no longer stigmatized. Emotions are much easier to discuss and access when they are accepted, and there is no better way to show tacit acceptance than by addressing them alongside musical principles. This will put your group at ease when emotions are in play, both in rehearsal and later in performance.

EMPOWERING LANGUAGE

As we look ahead into the next century,
leaders will be those who empower others.
—BILL GATES

We are often not aware of the specific words we use to communicate, but small changes in our vocabulary and approach can have a large impact. To this end, music directors can better empower and inform their choirs using the following techniques:

- Speak clearly and directly without making yourself part of the creative process. Don't say, "I want" or "I need you to get louder here" but rather simply, "Get louder in this passage." This makes it about the music, not about the director.
- Within reason, explain why certain choices are being made. An increase in volume might be to reinforce a lyric or support the soloist approaching a high note. People are more effective when they know why they are doing something.
- Give specific compliments rather than general praise, as it helps singers understand what they have done well and reinforces good technique.
- Do not be afraid to point out errors, but never ridicule. People are not trying to make mistakes.
- Do not falsely compliment the group. Be honest in your critiques and your praise. If something was good but not great, say it was good but not great. Singers will come to trust every word.
- Give singers an opportunity to self-critique. "What was better about that run-through?" "How did the chord sound after the change?" Sometimes your singers will make exactly the point you hoped they would, and sometimes they'll point out something else valuable.
- Give your singers an opportunity to make meaningful choices in rehearsal: "What song would you like to work on next?" "What should we sing in the concert this weekend?" "Should

we take a break or push through?" The decision won't always be what every member wants, but they'll respect both the democratic nature of the decision and the fact that you solicited their opinion.

- Expect the singers to do what you ask. They will rise to the occasion.
- Admit mistakes. People respond well to and respect leadership that is confident yet able to change course when necessary.

THE RIGHT WORDS

You cannot create results. You can only create conditions
in which something might happen.
—ANNE BOGART

Once the notes are learned and the details are cemented, the director's job is to help the singers perform at their peak level every time the song is sung, regardless of circumstance.

Embodying the proper emotion is central to this task, and inspiring the singers to follow suit is the logical next step. Directors will be tempted to say things like "Make it bigger!" "Give me more!" "Show it on your faces!" but these kinds of phrases are counterproductive. Why? Because your job is to help them connect to real emotion, not simply to exaggerate their facial expressions but to go deeper into their feelings.

Have you ever had someone tell you to feel a different emotion? Probably for as long as you have memories. Has it ever worked? No. If your parents admonished you for feeling sad, it didn't immediately make you happy, nor does it work for a friend to tell you, "Don't be angry." We can't alter another's mood by telling that person what to feel. Language is powerful, but it's not a scalpel when you wield it like a hammer.

Address your singers' thoughts, their feelings, their process, the communal act of expressing, but don't ask for more, bigger, better. If you're in need of more convincing, return to the fable printed at the very beginning of the book. Be the sun, not the wind.

ERODING INHIBITIONS

So many people out there can probably sing very good—
all they need to do is just drop their inhibitions.
That's why most people do their singing in the shower.
—GREGG ALLMAN

A variety of inhibitions can stand in the way of expressive singing. You may know:

- Introverted singers who are generally shy or afraid to express themselves in front of a crowd
- Perfectionistic singers who are focused on the notes and view any technical imperfection as worse than a lack of expression
- Stiff singers who are disconnected from their bodies and therefore don't express emotion on their faces
- Theatrical singers who use character to hide themselves and therefore express falsely, with exaggerated facial expressions and other melodramatic effects

People of different ages, backgrounds, and cultures will vary in their comfort with emotional expression, and any may exhibit a range of inhibitions. There is no single technique or magic formula that will address and eliminate them all, but you will find that a culture of openness in your group coupled with your addressing specific issues as they arise will help. In time, as your singers discover the look and feel of a healthy performing environment and ethos, you should find most of these inhibitive idiosyncrasies falling away. The remainder can be addressed individually, one-on-one, ideally at a time other than rehearsal when the individual can relax and not feel defensive or singled out.

Be careful not to erase all of a person's unique personality traits. There is not only one way to be emotional, and honesty isn't always pretty or uniform. Sometimes it's a little awkward, a little peculiar. That's a good thing. Variety is what makes a vocal harmony group compelling and gives it character. Work with your singers to get them all out of their shells, and once that happens, don't tinker too much. Let your group be themselves.

EMOTIONAL INTELLIGENCE

There is no separation of mind and emotions;
emotions, thinking, and learning are all linked.
—ERIC JENSEN

In 1995, psychologist Daniel Goleman wrote the book *Emotional Intelligence*, which popularized a new way of thinking about emotion. Emotional Intelligence (EI) is considered a measure of one's ability to identify emotions in oneself and others, to differentiate between emotions, and to use this information to guide thought and action.

Since its publication, several studies have shown that a high EI correlates with leadership, mental health, and job performance. In fact, EI has been shown to be twice as important as technical expertise or IQ in successful leadership.[1]

Experts disagree as to the nature of EI, some considering it an ability, others a trait. Some consider it to have little predictive power; others balk at it being considered its own intelligence. The scientific and social impact of EI remains unsettled, but it can be valuable for our purposes to consider the suite of qualities or skills that Goldman posits in his model:

- Emotional self-awareness
- Emotional self-regulation
- Social skills
- Empathy
- Motivation

Emotional intelligence has also been explained in terms of the ability to

- Perceive emotion
- Understand emotion

---

1   Daniel Goleman, *Working with Emotional Intelligence* (London: Bloomsbury, 1998).

- Use emotion
- Manage emotion

These categories can be useful in considering the ways in which emotion affects our lives, and how we may be stronger in one area than another. Without a standard definition or a standard means of measuring EI, it remains impossible for us to codify it for our purposes. Nonetheless, it pays to be aware of science's growing interest in the topic of emotion, and of how much we still don't know. If nothing else, it can be a useful topic for discussion among members of your group, in an ongoing quest to follow scientific and sociological research into emotion. Without a doubt, much will be learned in the years following the publication of this book, hopefully some of it directly applicable to good, connected emotional singing.

INNER CRITIC

Perfection is no more a requisite to art than to heroes.
Frigidaires are perfect. Beauty limps. My Frigidaire
has had to be replaced.
—NED ROREM

It is almost impossible to have made it to adulthood in modern culture without having developed your own inner critic. This voice in your head tells you when you are about to do something wrong and keeps you from making choices that could harm yourself and/or others. Usually this critic is beneficial, but occasionally it can stand in the way of excellent expressive singing.

Above all, our critic does not want us to do anything foolish. We've been socialized to believe that expressing emotion in most social situations is inappropriate, so it reminds us not to share our feelings publicly. This well-intentioned internal advice keeps us from singing with emotional power, so it must be silenced or overridden.

Additionally, our critic does not want us to look foolish. Facial expressions, body movements . . . in most cases it warns us to err on the side of less, so we walk down the street with no expression at all, refrain from dancing when we hear music, and so on. Music wants movement and facial engagement, so again we must disregard the critic's advice. When we're making music, we must physicalize it, or else we'll look stiff and disengaged.

Our critic looks to others in our immediate surroundings to gauge what is right at any given moment. The result? No one wants to step out of line, resulting in a sea of blank faces, a choir that reverts to the lowest common denominator. You may need to actively override your instinct to "follow the fold" and push yourself to disregard your critic when you look around the room and see people disengaged or afraid of emotion. It will likely feel uncomfortable at first, but if no one pushes against these instincts, nothing will change. Your bravery will be rewarded not only by your own powerful performance; it will lead the way for the entire group.

In many cases, a person with a firm inner critic is a person who would consider herself a "perfectionist." That person needs to constantly remind herself that singing without emotion is far from perfection.

PHYSICALITY

Music is the movement of sound to reach the soul
for the education of its virtue.
—Plato

Choreography is not a necessary component of emotionally impactful performances. In many cases, no choreography is more powerful, as sometimes choreography can get in the way of a song's mood or message. This does not mean that a choir should stand absolutely still while singing. On the contrary: just as singers must be free to move their mouths, eyes, and faces, so should they be free to allow their bodies to react to the music they are creating.

This can take several forms:

- Natural body movements (leaning, arm gestures) that arise from the act of singing
- Snapping or clapping, when appropriate to the piece
- Toe-tapping, knee bobbing, or other repetitive time-keeping pulse, which helps the singer remain locked into the groove
- Swaying or rocking
- A simple step-touch move (especially effective in gospel)
- Head turns to shift focus (on the lead singer, director, other singers, etc.)
- Simple blocking/staging, which can include standing, sitting, and other simple movements

And so on. Remember that the purpose of any movement in music is to reinforce and enhance the moment, mood, and message, which does not always equate to exacting physical precision. In the same way that we're all different, we all move differently, and that natural flow on stage reinforces a singer's instincts. Our bodies naturally align with our feelings if we let them, and teaching singers to be physically engaged when they sing will benefit your sound as well as the visual impact of your performance. A physically stiff choir, even when moving in unison, is rarely an emotionally expressive one.

In rehearsal, when standing, work on a healthy "neutral" stance: feet shoulder-width apart, back straight but not stiff, weight on the balls of the feet, knees and arms relaxed (not locked), torso flexible to allow for maximum breathing.

There are times when you'll need to reign in a singer who is particularly physical, or engage one who is particularly stiff. You're not looking for complete uniformity, but unbridled variety won't serve your mission, either. Much can be solved with the use of a video camera, allowing singers to self-regulate as they see how their movement fits into the larger picture.

The amount of appropriate movement depends on the song. An old folk ballad varies greatly from a 1970s disco medley. There are times when stillness is reflected in the music—and should likewise be reflected on stage. Common sense will guide you, and if in doubt, ask your group what feels natural.

Often when working with high school or collegiate ensembles I find them positioned single file in a wide arc across the stage, with the soloist in the middle (if any). In this formation, singers tend to look uncomfortable moving, exposed and uncertain, like the first person on the dance floor. When I begin to work with these singers, I compare that empty dance floor at a wedding to the crowded dance floor later the same night and remind them how much more comfortable they feel moving when close to one another. Then I bring them into a tight double arc, shoulder to shoulder, with people on the ends facing each other (e.g., a 13-member group would be perhaps 8 in the back row and 5 in the front) and have them repeat the song.

The difference is immediate: they can hear each other much better in this formation, and they're much more comfortable moving. This was the default formation for my college a cappella group, the Tufts Beelzebubs, and remains to this day an excellent fallback formation for pop a cappella ensembles of 9 to 20 members.

PRIORITIES

What comes from the mouth goes to the ear,
but what comes from the heart goes to the heart.
—Ancient Hindu proverb

Although movement can help a group's overall performance (rhythm, energy, unity), it's important to remember that people don't need to see music to feel it. Emotional honesty does not impact the audience's experience only via visual cues and facial expressions. Paul Ekman, as outlined in his book *Emotions Revealed*, studied and found that people can hear the emotions in others, even if they can't see them: "The voice is every bit as important as the face."

This shouldn't be a revelation when you consider that we experience most music via audio recording, be it over the radio, on our phones, in elevators and grocery stores and the like. We are impressed once by a musician's technical prowess, but we come back because we feel something.

With everything we do in life there are priorities, and it is the same with music. First of all comes the song's message and mood, which should at all times be your highest priority. If you're delivering a speech, you need to make sure the words are understood first and foremost, and that they're felt. Secondly, there are aesthetic considerations to the music that help support the message. These are good and important, but should never stand in the way of your message. Don't hold a pretty chord just because it's pretty if it will risk unraveling the song's message and effect. And finally there are all of the ancillary elements of a performance: wardrobe, lights, movement, and perhaps video projections and the like. These must integrate with your song's message, lest they be distracting or confusing.

If at any point you're not sure, less is more. Those recordings you love? Think of how deeply they move you through sound alone. If you put enough heart and truth into your singing, that will be all anyone else will need.

CALIBRATION

"But I never looked like that!" How do you know?
What is the "you" you might or might not look like?
—ROLAND BARTHES

A t this point you and your singers have taken many steps toward powerful, emotional singing. But how do individual performances within the group compare to one another? How does your group appear as a unit? Just as an engine needs to be set to run at the right speed, just as a scale needs to be set so that one pound equals one pound, so do you need to make sure your level of expression roughly matches that of your fellow singers and is coming across to the audience as you desire.

Mismatched levels of intensity can be distracting. Big facial expressions from one singer and almost imperceptibly subtle movements from the next can render both ineffective. Too much and you look fake, too little and you look bored or disengaged. There's no single proper level of energy, and there's no need for everyone to be at exactly the same level, but just as you can't have one person whisper beside another who is yelling, you want to make sure you're emoting within the same general framework.

When you look at the group as a whole, you want the effect to be both unified and effective. Sometimes the problem is not a mismatch within the group but rather that the entire group is too reserved and subtle. Every season of *The Sing-Off*, there was some group that thought they were giving more than they were. I would mention this to them and they'd look at me like I was crazy, insisting, "We feel like we're being clownishly huge in our facial expressions!" So I'd take them to a monitor during rehearsal playback and show them what they actually looked like. "Oh!" they'd exclaim. "Got it!"—and in the next run-through they were at the right level. They did not need to express dishonestly; they just needed to see that what they thought they were giving was not what was being received.

Then there was the occasional performer who was used to a live musical theater setting and would give too much for the television cameras. It took no more than one viewing for that person to bring it back in line with the others. In these cases, a moving picture is worth a thousand words.

There are two ways to make sure your group is properly calibrated:

1. **Mirror.** Have your group sing into a mirror, ideally a large one, if you're near a dance studio or similar room, so you don't have to strain to see yourselves. This can be very telling but can only get you so far, as you're singing for yourselves, not others, and analyzing while you do it, so the levels are likely not exactly what you'll give on stage.[1]
2. **Video.** Rehearsal video can be helpful, but there's nothing better than performance video, where you can see how people perform with full engagement and full volume in front of an audience. As much as singers may try to bring performance-level intensity to a rehearsal, it's just not the same. If possible, get the camera up close enough so you can see people's faces, and perhaps film with multiple cameras. Don't get lost in the forest and nitpick every eye twitch and curled lip; instead use the video to get an overall picture of how your group is emoting, person to person and song to song.

---

1 Mirrors can be powerful and bring up feelings, especially when singers are in a state of emotional openness and vulnerability. During my sixth week of *Pitch Slapped*, I wanted the stage picture to be a line of women putting on makeup before prom, and one singer (Sam) was just not able to look at herself as she sang. You never know when something emotional will come up, and when it does, it's often best to address it right away, which we did, bringing the group closer together and giving Sam the confidence she needed to be one of the group's most emotional performers.

OVERBOARD

Too much of a good thing can be taxing.
—MAE WEST

There are two ways that emotional performing can go beyond impactful and become off-putting.

The first is if the performances are emotional to the point of becoming melodramatic. Just as a movie needs to "earn" its emotional scenes, so must you build naturally and honestly to your group's emotional peaks. To dive head first into angry hostility or heart-wrenching weeping can be more distancing than compelling. To avoid this, program your performances to build emotionally, each song growing in intensity, rather than starting with the darkest, most challenging performance. If in doubt, it always works to start with a joyful, inviting song.

The second problem arises when artists put too much emphasis on weighty emotions. There are bands and solo artists who are known for their insight into the darker side of the human psyche, but an a cappella group, especially a scholastic group, is rarely of the proper maturity and temperament to believably deliver consistently negative messages. Nowhere has the prevalence of the dark side of humanity been more explored in a cappella than in the International Championship of Collegiate A Cappella in recent years. With time for only a few songs and a desire to make an impact on the judges and audience, several collegiate groups have created sets that start dark and stay dark. They're not always unsuccessful, but on balance they're far less believable than groups that show a range of emotions. Collegiate a cappella is fun, so a performance that entirely avoids that central feeling appears disingenuous. Moreover, rarely are the students able to sustain such negativity. Instead, since they're determined, they double down, which leads to insincere, overwrought performing.

In the same way that you look at a group's vocal range and personality when choosing songs, so should you consider their general temperament. Songs of loss, sorrow, anger, and confusion absolutely have their place in a cappella, but rarely is it appropriate for them to be a group's norm.

OVERWHELM

I think people who are artists, actors, singers, great songwriters,
they tend to have a hyper state of emotion
where they feel things very, very deeply, probably more deeply
than the average person walking down the street.
—WILLIE AAMES

It is inevitable that a focus on emotionally difficult issues will at times result in emotional overload, especially with a group of singers not used to conjuring and harnessing their feelings.

The first thing to know and to make sure your group understands is that this is absolutely normal. People cry. This is not a bad thing, and it is not something that a group that shares feelings should shy away from. A couple of tears may fall during a rehearsal without negatively affecting a singer's ability to perform. If the tears become more powerful, it should be known that it's all right for the singer to stop singing and take some time before reentering. If the feelings are overwhelming and not easily subdued, it's all right if the singer steps away from the group, finds a quiet corner, and rejoins the group when ready.

The more your singers practice with honest emotion, the better they'll individually be able to exercise the "muscle" that releases and harnesses their emotions. Like the gas pedal on a car, one can lean into or pull back on the emotion as needed, but at first this is very difficult, especially if the song requires consideration of feelings of loss or death.

To know you're supported, to know that expressing emotion is healthy, to know that your fellow singers are also on the same quest all makes it easier to take a risk, and less embarrassing should one become overwhelmed. Make it clear during rehearsals that emotional overwhelm might happen. When it does, react with empathy and grace, yet don't let it derail your music rehearsal. You're all there to make music, and to stop making music is to send the message that emotions have the power to disrupt everyone's experience, which only intensifies the fear and embarrassment around becoming overwhelmed. In time, emotional access will become second nature, your singers will be respectful of the occasional overwhelm, and it will all become a normal part of your group's culture and musical process.

RECHARGE

I bought some batteries, but they weren't included.
—STEVEN WRIGHT

People all started to sing for a reason, be it because they love music, love the stage, love connecting with others, or all three. Alas, there are times when we fall into a rut, forget why we're doing something, and need a reminder, a jolt of energy from jumper cables.

At times like these, I recommend you take the group outside its comfort zone. Go sing for some people for whom live music will make a big difference. Maybe it's a senior home, maybe it's a women's shelter, maybe it's a halfway house or a prison.

If you're having trouble finding places like this to perform, there may be organizations in your area that can help. For instance, Bread and Roses, formed by Mimi Fariña (Joan Baez's sister), provides 600 performances each year across Northern California in locations with people who don't have an opportunity or ability to go hear live music (http://www.breadandroses.org). Or you can just call local organizations and see if a free concert would be welcome.

Along the same lines, there are some choirs that exist explicitly for this purpose. Threshold choirs (http://thresholdchoir.org) sing at the bedsides of those on the threshold of life, either about to give birth or to die.

If your singers are not feeling a connection to the music or to the audience, if they seem burned out, if they're having trouble caring, I recommend you take them into an environment where they'll feel the connection immediately, where the act of performing might initially be a struggle but they'll leave with a renewed sense of the power of vocal harmony.

While filming *Pitch Slapped* I wanted the singers in Stay Tuned to step away from focusing on competitions and remember what matters about music, so I brought them to a local family shelter. The room was full of young children, mothers embarrassed to be seen and filmed in such circumstances—and yet when the singing started, the room transformed, the children danced, a weight was lifted.

Do not forget what a powerful gift you have, and do not hesitate to give it away to people who most need it. What you get in return will be far more valuable than money.

Motivations

MUSICAL MOTIVATION

Motivation is the fuel, necessary to keep the human engine running.
—ZIG ZIGLAR

Composers and arrangers know what they want technically and emotionally, and their choices in the score, from pitches and rhythms to dynamics and articulation, all serve this purpose. Legato phrases feel different from staccato notes, slow notes from fast notes, and even fast loud staccato notes from fast quiet staccato notes—one perhaps reminiscent of thundering down the stairs and the other of quickly tiptoeing down a hall. The choices made in music notation have been "translated" from feelings and real life, and when you accurately reproduce them you're breathing life back into the sheet music, reconstituting the emotions that inspired the notes on the page.

When discussing musical choices with your group, ground them in emotion. Every crescendo and sforzando, every rubato and fermata, every articulation you take from the score and those you impose yourself are part of a master plan, and that master plan is to create music that is beautiful, powerful, meaningful.

Your singers can sing loudly if you tell them to, but if you explain to them why a passage should be loud, if they can connect the dynamics to the moment to the meaning to the emotion, their loudness will be more grounded, more focused, more reliable. They will own it, as it becomes a part of the way they tell a story. With apologies to fishermen everywhere: Give a man a dynamic and he will sing loudly once; teach a man why the dynamics are there and he will sing the passage loudly for a lifetime.

PERFORMING AS DIRECTOR

If your actions inspire others to dream more, learn more, do more,
and become more, you are a leader.
—JOHN QUINCY ADAMS

What does a performer do? Stand in front of a room full of people and command their attention, present something beautiful, offer insights, create understanding, take the audience on an emotional journey, and enrich their lives. That is exactly what a director should do.

Directors should look at the podium as a stage, their singers as an audience. Every word, gesture, comment has meaning and power. It is not enough just to drag yourself to rehearsal and stumble through the music relying on your instinct and experience. You need to make the moment special for the singers, make rehearsal a place they want to be, a place they leave full of knowledge and with a sense of satisfaction.

Moreover, directors control the mood of a room. Having a bad day? Leave it at the door. When you enter the rehearsal, bring the level of energy and excitement that you want your singers to have. When the song changes, your energy should change accordingly. If you want to draw sadness from your singers to reinforce the lyrics, you too need to embody that emotion. Show, don't tell.

This can be exhausting, but it is also deeply rewarding.

LEADING FROM THE FRONT

A leader is best when people barely know he exists.
When his work is done, his aim fulfilled,
they will say: we did it ourselves.
—LAO TZU

Much of the work in this book requires an instigator and a vanguard: someone to explain the processes and someone to demonstrate their effectiveness. The expression "do as I say, not as I do" will not work in this circumstance. If you want everyone in your group to embrace emotional singing, then you must practice what you preach, which means you will usually be first: first to share your feelings, first to sing with emotion, first to come across the various roadblocks you will collectively encounter.

Perhaps the single least talked about and yet most valuable trait for a vocal director is charisma. This charisma is useful in convincing people to join the group, to stay late in rehearsal, to work hard, to prioritize their music. These are all important, yet a leader's charisma is perhaps most valuable when it comes to focusing a group's emotional understanding and performance of a song. These moments can be very tense, fragile, uncertain. Group members will not know how to respond, being in a new situation, a public evaluation of emotional issues. This is the time, more than any, that group leaders, directors and otherwise, should be out in front: expressing, sharing, gently steering the dialogue to the right level of intensity and depth, carefully bringing the entire experience in for a smooth landing. This doesn't require perfection, only care and preparation.

Note that a director cannot and should not be expected to conduct emotion during a rehearsal or performance. To lead emotionally does not mean a conductor should try to pull the emotions out of the group. Just as saying, "Be sadder!" or "More joy!" is completely ineffectual, so is it impossible for a director to try through a combination of arm gestures and facial expressions to elicit or amplify emotions from a group. While conducting, any facial expressions should only be honest, real, connected to the music. In this way a conductor is leading by example, showing what is possible without trying to force it out of the singers. This may seem a narrow distinction, but it is an essential one. As Yoda famously said, "Do or do not, there is no try." You can't try to get your singers to be more emotional, and you can't try to feel more emotion yourself. You can only use the techniques in this book to feel the emotion for yourself, and lead from the front.

LEAD VOCAL

Like all soul singers, I grew up singing in church,
but sometimes I would leave early and sit in the car listening to
the Blind Boys of Alabama. Hearing their lead singer Clarence
made me connect the idea of church and show business
and see how I could make a career singing music that stirred the soul.
—DARYL HALL

Watching a gospel choir in action can teach you a lot about the potential relationship between a vocal group and its soloist. There is an interplay, an energy and intensity the performers share, feeding off each other. So should it be with all vocal groups in all styles.

When we think of dynamic lead singers, we look at them in awe. What a tremendous voice, talent, and energy. We may not have their voice, but we can perform with just as much energy and have just as much fun. Why should Freddie Mercury be the only one allowed to prance around the stage? Why shouldn't other lead singers bring the same intensity that Madonna does? One of the most compelling things about a collegiate a cappella group is their energy and the fun they have. Unbridled from a faculty director for the first time in their young lives, collegiate a cappella singers sing the songs they want to sing the way they want to sing them. Moreover, they are living on their own away from their parents for the first time, and feel a freedom that they bring to the stage. There is no reason other groups can't match their intensity on background parts and on lead vocals, which, if sung with commitment, can spur all the performers to new heights . . . or wherever the song takes you.

POWERFUL MOMENTS

Every moment and every event of every man's life on earth
plants something in his soul.
—Thomas Merton

Ultimately a great concert is a series of great moments: wonderful pieces of music, each presented with a depth of understanding and conviction toward the song's meaning, message, and mood. A great album is the same way, song after song of poignancy, power, presence. This is what music is at its best—a reflection of life's most powerful moments.

It's likely that throughout this book you have been focusing on the songs and performances, how you can help convince, inspire, and lead your group to perform with emotional intensity to create powerful moments for your audience.

Taking a step back, shouldn't you look at your group the same way? Shouldn't your rehearsals, performances, and other times together be a series of powerful moments? Sure, not every day can be special (by definition), but use some of the energy you are putting into bringing your audience on a fantastic journey and focus it on ensuring that your group is on a fantastic journey together as well. Take time to appreciate the music you are creating. Celebrate your successes together. Pause and reflect from time to time. Make the group more than an occasional pastime; make it a gathering of friends.

I have created a cappella groups for both Disneyland and Disney World, and I was a bit shocked at first when I saw what these parks look like behind the scenes, backstage. It's not disgusting, but it's not nice, either: trailers, concrete, industrial, blah. All of the magic is focused toward the people who attend the park, and backstage, if it weren't for the Mickey Mouse posters, you'd think you were working at a Walmart warehouse. Don't let your group be like that, with all of the attention and energy directed outward. Save some of the best moments, the best energy for yourselves. Not only will it further motivate your singers to greater commitment in the future, it's simply the right thing to do. The intragroup harmony your singers experience will result in greater harmony on stage: harmony through harmony.

At this point in the book you should have a good understanding of the reason emotion matters in music and how it can be drawn forth from lyrics, honestly conjured and crafted in rehearsal, then presented on stage in concert with the other singers in your group.

I could end the book here, but I feel there is more insight to be gleaned from the experiences of a variety of different directors, coaches, singers, and arrangers who are known for their success with and sensitivity to this topic.

Insights

All emotion is involuntary when genuine.
—MARK TWAIN

The act of connecting emotionally to music while performing is a very personal one, and each person's process and journey are unique. In order to present a range of perspectives in these pages, I decided to interview key members of the vocal music community in a variety of fields whose experiences have been powerful and whose music has been very emotionally effective. My questions are intentionally wide ranging in hopes of uncovering each person's specific accumulated knowledge. During this dragnet I uncovered some excellent pointers not directly related to emotion in music but nonetheless valuable, which I decided to include as well: your unexpected vocal harmony bycatch. Good advice is good advice regardless of where you find it.

COMPOSERS

Before literature, before theater, before visual arts, there was music, which makes composition the earliest art form of the human race. This stands to reason, as we are musical creatures, born to sing. Styles of music have changed throughout human history, and yet one constant remains: the primacy of the human voice. These composers are all known for creating powerful contemporary works built in and around vocal harmony.

Christopher Tin

Some composers are born into families filled with vocal harmony, and others stumble upon it later. Christopher Tin falls in the latter camp, but since he found vocal music it has never left him, forming the core of a sound and style that circles the globe. With both critical and popular success, blending styles modern and ancient, local and international, his style is universal yet never loses the unique nature of each component tradition, like a delicious recipe in which you can taste each distinct element.

DEKE SHARON: You were very involved in music before and during college. What drew you to a cappella?

CHRISTOPHER TIN: I sang in choir my senior year of high school and enjoyed it from both a musical and social perspective. While it was fun singing madrigals and such, when I got to Stanford and saw that there were self-run groups singing gospel, R&B, and world music, it really blew my mind. I'd heard a lot about this group Talisman before I arrived on campus, and so I immediately went to audition, and to my surprise I was accepted. For me, singing a cappella wasn't about performance, choreography, skits, or shows. It was just about the singing. I didn't care whether we ever did a single concert or not. I just liked being in a room full of people harmonizing.

DS: You won a Grammy for "Baba Yetu," the first video game theme ever nominated. How did your work with Stanford Talisman inform that composition?

CT: My time singing and music directing Talisman had a huge influence on my own compositional style. Prior to Stanford, I had very little exposure to world music, much less African gospel. Singing all that African music really embedded certain musical gestures and forms in me—call and response, rhythmic and repetitive homophonic chords, etc. Directing Talisman was in essence my extracurricular study while I was doing a composition degree and learning to conduct and write for the orchestra. All these influences came into play when I was asked to write the theme for *Civilization IV*, which ultimately became the song "Baba Yetu."

DS: Your first album, *Calling All Dawns*, features a variety of styles of vocal music, including African choral music, opera, medieval chants, and Irish keening. What draws you to feature vocal harmony so prominently in your compositions?

CT: It's in my DNA. I love vocals—the richer, the better. I'm generally pretty fascinated by the different sounds that singers around the world use—everything from guttural throat singing to the warm blend of a classical choir. Having been a singer myself, I know just how powerful of a feeling it is to be singing in a group. There's just something amazing about standing side by side with your peers and singing your heart out. There's a warm feeling of community that's unlike anything else in music.

DS: Your latest song cycle features 10 songs in 10 different languages, including Sanskrit, Xoxha, Mongolian, and ancient Greek. Why do you work with so many languages, and what have you learned about directing choirs that sing in languages they don't speak?

CT: The reason my big song cycles feature so many languages is in part that there's a bit of a unifying cross-cultural message that's implicit throughout. The biggest challenge, however, is getting non-native choirs to reproduce what the authentic singers do. This is particularly challenging with some vocal traditions, like Bulgarian women's choirs, but I've found that a lot of singers rise to the challenge and seem to embrace it. Most classical choral literature is performed in the same way—with nice, rounded vowels, warm tones, blend . . . a nice, homogeneous sound. It's a sound I love, but at the same time, I often yearn for something different. In the process of having my music performed, I've discovered that a lot of choirs out there are eager to try something different as well.

DS: What have you learned from working with vocal harmony groups as diverse as Anonymous 4 and the Soweto Gospel Choir? What elements are universal; what should all choirs know?
CT: There's very little that groups as different as Anonymous 4 and the Soweto Gospel Choir share in common, and it's impossible to find a one-size-fits-all approach in working with them. But all singers feel in their hearts the desire to express something through their singing, and often you as a vocal producer just have to take a hands-off approach and let them tackle the material in the manner that they're comfortable with. Likewise, you have to understand the psychology of working with singers. You have to know that a happy singer produces a nice sound, and an inspired singer produces an inspired performance. So one of your principal jobs as a vocal producer is just to make singers feel like at that moment, they're the most gifted and amazing singers in the world. That's how you get a good performance out of them.

Tat Tong

Though you likely don't know his name, Tat Tong is one of the world's most successful young songwriters. He has over 200 original pop songs on albums around the world, 17 platinum records, and over 50 Top 20 hits, including 20 number one hits worldwide. And where did he get his start? Cornell's a cappella group Last Call, where he first learned to produce vocals, engineer, arrange, and mix. Before becoming a worldwide sensation, Tat was a darling of the a cappella community, with creative remixes that blurred the line between a cappella and electronica. Now he's signed to Universal Music Publishing and makes up half of the hit-making team the Swaggernautz.

DEKE SHARON: You've written hit songs in 66 countries in four different languages (English, Mandarin, Cantonese, Spanish). Do you find there are any differences in the way you write an effective song for different music markets or in different languages? Are the messages and the emotions universal?

TAT TONG: Through my journey in writing music, I've learned that there are no absolutes. All art sits in a culturally specific context, and that definitely applies to hit songs in different markets as well. It's important to appreciate the differences between markets to be effective in creating songs that labels, artists, and their audiences will love.

For melody, globalization has done its job in exposing audiences around the world to the predominant American and European pop paradigm, and this is where I feel there is most common ground between the tastes of audiences in different territories. What is hot in America tends to become popular (after some delay) in the rest of the world. But even so, there are differences—for example, the American hit melodies are now driven more by groove than by long, beautiful lines, which tend to sound dated or cheesy in the U.S. market. On the flip side, Asian and Latin audiences tend to crave these very melodies, and something that is overly groove-based at the expense of melodic beauty does not fare well in those markets. Also, some markets like Japan currently prefer songs in major over minor modes, whereas many American pop songs tend to be in minor to be more edgy.

For lyrics, local considerations take over almost completely. The kinds of rhythms that sound good and make sense sung in each language will to a large extent dictate the groove of the melody. For example, when writing in Mandarin or Japanese, it is important to have enough syllables to allow for meaningful lyrics to be written, but a melody constructed this way may sound overly wordy when paired with English lyrics. Also, vowel sounds in each language differ, and especially on high belted notes, some languages like Spanish with big open vowels sound much better and are easier to sing than English with its more closed vowels. Also, you have to consider what lingo is "street" and cool, and what messages are relevant—which also differs completely with territory, yet plays a critical role in having the song resonate with a younger audience.

For example, drugs, violence, and sex are cool in the American urban rap genre but would not be as accepted by audiences in China. And writing about love in flowery, poetic phrases may be de rigeur in Latin or Japanese ballads, but the same approach would probably make current American audiences cringe. As someone who has spent a ton of time in America but is still not a local, I lean heavily on my cowriters, particularly my writing partner Jovany in the Swaggernautz, to provide me with this cultural insight and context when we are dealing with genres that require such lyrics.

All this technical and cultural stuff aside, at our very core we are all humans, and what we want from music is the same: to make us laugh, cry, reminisce, think, and come to terms with our life situations. In this sense, the emotions conveyed by music are more or less universal across cultures. And the best part about working in so many markets is that through the process of writing music, I gain a really deep insight into the psyche of each culture as well.

DS: You sang a cappella in college and cut your teeth as an engineer, producer, arranger, and mixer for a cappella groups. What lessons did you learn from a cappella?

TT: So many! To start, I pretty much owe my production abilities—vocal production, mixing, mastering—to a cappella. If not for my group Cornell Last Call needing to complete an album on a tight budget, I'd never have learned to do those things, or made the many mistakes along the way that are essential to leveling up my skills. Through arranging a cappella, I learned to hear intricate vocal harmonies in my head, which has come in very handy in my mainstream pop work now, when I have to construct a background vocal stack with the artist in the studio on the fly. And my experiences with amateur collegiate singers of varying abilities (a.k.a. my baptism of fire)—having to coax them into delivering their best vocal performances, using all the psychological tricks I had at my disposal, and then often working in Melodyne to fix blend and tuning—have also put me in a great position to vocally produce the pop singers I work with today.

On the production/mixing front, my approach and aesthetic from the start was to push way past the boundaries of what sounded "vocal"—to create timbres and textures reminiscent of instrumental music. Having so little timbral variety to work with in the typical collegiate arrangement/performance, I quickly learned that I needed to be able to "hear" the finished product in my head, and then use all the tools at my disposal to morph and mess with the vocals to get as close as possible to my vision. In retrospect, a lot of my earlier mixes feel kind of gimmicky to me now, but all that practice imagining the final sound and using a ton of different plug-ins to turn vocals into something completely different and cool sounding, made it way easier to transition into instrumental arranging and production when the time came.

I do need to give a shout-out to [legendary a cappella producer] Bill Hare here. The week in 2004 that he graciously let me stay at his house, eating his food, driving his car, and watching him mix the Cartoon Johnny record on a seriously limited time frame was very much a pivotal moment for me as a mixing engineer and producer, and I still use a lot of the tips that I learned that week in my day-to-day work.

Also very important: a cappella taught me how to deal with the egos of over a dozen singers at once, as well as my own. I was never the best singer in the group, and I would frequently be disappointed when I didn't get the coveted solo spot I wanted for a song I loved. I like to think that all that rejection gave me the skin of a rhinoceros, which is always useful now that I'm in the mainstream music industry.

DS: To turn it around, what lessons have you learned now that you're an international hit songwriter that apply to vocal music?
TT: As mainstream pop songwriters, we have to be very sensitive to what will connect with the audience, what will draw them into a song in the first 10 to 30 seconds, and, on the flip side, what will distract them and make them tune out. A strong melody with multiple hooks, followed by lyrics that listeners can read their own circum-

stances into, are key. Once you have these, the productions surrounding the all-important lead vocal are often surprisingly simple with at most five or six elements in the climax of the song; any more would be distracting and undermine the power of the song.

Too often in a cappella (especially collegiate), I feel the focus is backwards—on "cool" background syllables or clever chords or other musical intricacies, and (when live) flamboyant choreography, instead of the lead vocal and its nuances. From a larger perspective, I feel that a cappella's cool factor (all voices, no safety net) is also its Achilles heel: too much focus on the form and highlighting its coolness and artistry can detract from communicating the substance of the song—what it's trying to say—which is everything when connecting with an audience. In that regard, I feel that Pentatonix's new album is an excellent example of paring back the bells and whistles to allow mainstream audiences to easily get what they need from the music, and hence connect with it.

Lastly, in the mainstream pop world, sound trends and genres come and go, and it's important as a creative to be ahead of the curve just enough to stand out while not alienating audiences. I'm not entirely sure how this would apply to a cappella, but perhaps coming up with new ways of layering or texturing syllables, or new types of vocal percussion sounds, might work to establish a fresh, interesting sonic language that could potentially become a trend.

DS: What comments do you find yourself making to singers most often?
TT: Breathe. Relax. Keep it nice and open. We'll do as many takes as you need. More air!

DS: With your finger on the pulse of so many music markets, how can vocal groups create music recordings and videos that have the maximum impact globally?
TT: We've already discussed the musical aspects of a worldwide hit, so let's focus on something that I think a lot of indie a cappella groups leave out: marketing. For maximum impact, it's important not to assume that simply uploading killer music will ensure a huge audience overnight. The Internet is beyond saturated, and audiences these days have a shockingly low attention span. I'm no expert, but the idea is this: if you're spending six months to a year making your album, expect to spend just as much time and effort (not to mention money) marketing it. It's a painstaking job

to identify your audience, create the correct image and content for your act, reel listeners in, and convert them to fans—and the big online platforms like Facebook already charge users to give their posts the desired reach. So my advice would be to budget accordingly.

Likewise, I don't really feel qualified to comment on videos, but I feel like the whole multi-panel, one-man band–style video trend is beyond passé now. Everyone out there is familiar with the concept, and the Internet has a really short attention span. This is analogous to my previous point on highlighting the form too much over the substance. Going back to basics, Nils Gums, a good friend and manager of Karmin, always talks about the principle of a "purple cow," something people just can't take their eyes off. Whether it's a galloping Asian dude á la Gangnam Style, or a pooping unicorn á la the Squatty Potty ads, something visually new is something people will talk about and share.

Eric Whitacre

If you had to name the biggest rock star in contemporary choral composition, there's no contest: it's Eric Whitacre. Drawing on a wide range of influences, he writes dense, sonorous choral music that appeals to insiders and laypeople alike. Through his significant online presence and ubiquitous appearance on every list of modern choral repertoire, his work has had a significant impact on the sound and direction of modern harmony.

DEKE SHARON: You write instrumental music as well, yet you're perhaps best known for your vocal works. Why do you think your choral music is so well received by people, including young singers?

ERIC WHITACRE: I honestly have no idea! I would like to think that it is because the music, and the poetry I choose, is truthful and authentic. (At least, I aspire to write music that is truthful and authentic). I spend a lot of time crafting every line so that each voice part feels important, feels like their part is musically and spiritually integral to the piece. Maybe that is what people are responding to? Also, I feel like I simply got lucky in terms of timing and was able to ride a wave of popularity for contemporary choral music that was really started by Arvo Pärt and Morten Lauridsen.

DS: Popular music is increasingly less harmonically and rhythmically complex, yet your successful works are a mélange of stacked seconds and mixed meters. How are you able to make such complexity compelling to a generation of people raised on four chords and four on the floor?

EW: I think it is all about context. The piece must very clearly teach its musical language to the audience and to the performers. It must be self-referential and self-contained, and adhere to its own laws. I call these pieces "snow globes," as if the entire universe of the piece is contained within that little globe. If a piece can successfully do that, then people will be happy to listen to and perform much more challenging music than they might otherwise do.

DS: Your virtual choirs have millions of views and tens of thousands of singers, a marriage of the latest technology and the oldest form of music. How did you reconcile these very different elements, and do you see continued successful marriages of choral music and technology happening?

EW: There is a Native American concept that I love: use the whole buffalo. The original American peoples would never dream of killing a buffalo and only taking its tongue and hide as European settlers would later do. They would use every part of the animal, its organs, its bones, its hooves. There is a great respect for the animal in this way that reflects a beautiful, elegant way of living within nature.

When it comes to creating things, I try and embrace this lesson. As I compose, *everything* is the buffalo. Anything I can see or touch becomes something to be used, something to be integrated into the music or work of art. With the Virtual Choir I was spending a lot of time watching choirs on YouTube, so YouTube and the Internet became a natural extension of the music and the concert hall. With my new piece Deep Field, in which the audience plays apps as the orchestra and choir perform, the smartphones in the audience became part of the buffalo.

I can't wait to see what new technologies will appear, and if I can get my hands on them they will undoubtedly find their way into my music.

DS: Prior to your best-selling albums, choral music was usually relegated to second-class status when compared to classical orchestral and instrumental music, even though the voice was the first instrument and our musical notation system was created for a cappella. Is there a reason for the resurgence of vocal music now?
EW: I believe singing together is fundamental to the human experience; people have been doing it in one way or another since the dawn of man.

DS: What tips do you have for writers and arrangers of vocal harmony music of all styles?
EW: I'm paraphrasing (no pun intended), but Schoenberg said something along the lines of "A perfect phrase is any group of notes that can be sung in a single breath." When writing vocal lines it's all about the breath: when to breathe, where to breathe, how to construct the perfect moment for the next breath. When I am writing I sing through every line in every part to make certain it connects to the breath and the body. If your vocal lines are natural and singable, the piece will unfold in an effortless and inevitable way.

DS: What are the most important things for directors to know when working with a vocal ensemble?

166

EW: It took me years to fully understand this, but the conductor must physically model a healthy singing posture for their choir. Relaxed shoulders, relaxed jaw, strong legs, low breath, bright eyes. Singers, more than any other performers, mirror the conductor, so the choir conductor's primary job must be to free their singers' bodies and let them sing!

ARRANGERS

Nowhere is the role of arranger more important than in vocal harmony. With rare exception, the human voice can only create one pitch at a time, so every moment of harmony needs to be carefully considered in advance. And these considerations need to simultaneously balance a group's range and technical ability with the song's overall emotional structure. There are thousands of notes and choices in every song, and creating a work that fits a group perfectly is a blend of science and art.

Ben Bram and Robert Dietz

Ben Bram and Robert Dietz are two of the most successful young arrangers today, and I've had the pleasure of working closely with them both. Ben Bram had won the International Championship of Collegiate A Cappella twice with the USC SoCal Vocals when I hired him to start working with me on *The Sing-Off*, and later we worked together on *Pitch Perfect*. He helped form Pentatonix and continues to arrange for and produce the group, garnering him several gold records and two Grammys.

I first met Robert Dietz when he was in high school, and was so impressed with his arranging that I published several of his songs. His high school albums both won Contemporary A Cappella Recording Awards (CARAs) for best high school album and best high school song. He made it to the International Championship of Collegiate A Cappella (ICCA) finals twice with Ithacappella, and won awards for best vocal percussion and best arrangement. He joined my *Sing-Off* team upon graduating college and remains one of a cappella's most in-demand arrangers and coaches. Together with Pentatonix's Avi Kaplan, Ben and Rob run A Cappella Academy.

DEKE SHARON: When did you each first start arranging? Why?
ROB DIETZ: I did my first arrangement at age 14 and got into it really

just out of necessity. My high school quintet wanted to do the Monkees' "I'm a Believer," and at the time if you wanted to cover a song a cappella, odds were good that you'd have to do the arrangement yourself. Back in 2002 there just wasn't the same access to a cappella sheet music or a cappella professionals that there is now. It was often DIY or not at all.

We started by recording three of us together improvising the song (live, one take, onto an ancient minidisk recorder), and then I took the ideas from that and fleshed them out into something a little more structured. The result was what I would call my first real "arrangement"—a crude but effective vocal sketch of the song.

BEN BRAM: My first memory of a complete written arrangement was age 14, though I had been noodling, recording, and experimenting long before that. The arrangement was also an original composition of mine, called *Iberian Suite*, written for brass quintet. I played French horn in the quintet, and the reason I composed this piece was to have something of mine to perform at the upcoming chamber music concert at my school. This desire to be useful, and to provide instrumentalists and vocalists with something exciting to play, is a key component of what still motivates me to arrange today.

RD: It's interesting thinking back on that first time now that this has become my profession. At that point, I don't even think I knew that what I was doing was called "arranging." It was just something that had to be done so that my group could perform the song we wanted to perform, in the way we wanted to do it. The reason for doing it, and the process we took to get there, was just about as organic as you can get.

DS: What did you learn, both positive and negative, from arrangements you sang when you were younger?

BB: One of the biggest things I learned was that I needed to make my arrangements fun to sing and play if I could at all help it. There was nothing worse than being bored and unsatisfied by the part you were given, especially if the overall experience was also unsatisfying to the listener. And of course, on the positive side, I was elated when I got a killer line, and always noticed good voice leading, a great harmonic moment, rhythmic interplay, and so many other awesome musical moments.

RD: Most of the pop stuff I sang from age 14 to 18 was my own—again, there just wasn't that much available (especially not for a quintet of high school dudes). I think that was both a blessing and a curse. On the plus side, I really got the opportunity to fail early and often, and to see my own material performed in front of a variety of different audiences (most of them appreciative, but many of them critical in their own ways). I don't think I was cognitively aware of it at the time, but looking back there's no doubt that seeing my work go through that feedback loop so many times helped form the foundation of the way that I think about arranging: from an audience's perspective. I remember vividly the feeling of being onstage singing something that didn't connect with the people in the room, and I try in all of my work to avoid that at all costs.

The negative was that I made a lot of mistakes that I might have avoided had I been exposed to a greater variety of quality material sooner. A lot of my knowledge of good part writing came from choral singing and feeling the ways in which vocal lines were woven together. I might have been able to glean more of that kind of information in the pop realm had more of that material been available. Some was, of course, but it was pretty much just the stuff that you [Deke] made available—my group did two: "Peace, Love, and Understanding" and "Dive into You" (which is still one of my favorite five-part arrangements).

It's interesting to think about what YouTube has done to budding arrangers (or artists in any field, really). I saw a comedian talk once about how he felt fortunate to get his start before the Internet boom, as nowadays everyone's first attempt at anything often goes straight online, into the crucible of potential ridicule. Nobody gets the luxury to fail in private, and if they do it's often short-lived. I wonder if I would have followed the same path had I not had the time that I did to refine my skills, free of the burden of comparison to others. I think there's a good chance I would have been discouraged early on, and maybe would have even given it up (or at the very least wouldn't have enjoyed the process of learning nearly as much as I did).

DS: To what extent does the emotional impact of the original version influence your choices as an arranger?

RD: The first decision I make when I'm sitting down with a new song is how I want the performance of my arrangement to affect the audience. If I want it to have a similar impact to what I think the original creates, then I'll often use a lot of the material that I think is effective from the original to evoke that effect. If I want to take it down a different path, then I'll often try to distance myself from the vibe of the original as much as possible in order to get myself into that alternate head space (sometimes going as far as to record a piano/guitar/vocal demo of my interpretation to work from instead).

BB: It depends on what kind of emotional impact you as the arranger choose to make with your arrangement. If your desired impact is similar or identical to the impact of the original version, then of course there will be lots of influence. There are times when an a cappella arrangement can improve upon and/or clarify the emotional impact of the original. When people say that a cover is "better than the original," I think this is what they're referring to: a clarity of vision, simplicity, a genuine and impeccable execution.

RD: There are two main things that guide my decision about which path to take: the core content of the song (main melodies and lyrics, mostly) and how well known the original song is. As far as the core content is concerned, I think you have to be careful not to try and fit a square peg into a round hole. Stevie Wonder's "Isn't She Lovely" probably isn't going to make the best heavy metal tune, because the core message of the song (celebrating the birth of a child and the love of family) doesn't really mesh with the head-banging mission statement of metal music. I'm not really interested in the ska "Change Is Gonna Come" or the ballad version of MJ's "Bad," either. You get the idea.

The other thing to consider is how familiar most people will be with the original, as you can get more mileage (and raise more ire) out of messing around with a classic. I typically only make big changes to classic tunes if I want to really throw the audience for a loop, I want to make a strong statement with an arrangement, or the changes don't break with the song's basic feel and are really more of an update for modern audience sensibilities than an outright overhaul of the material.

DS: How much does an arranger create and/or dictate emotion in an arrangement?
BB: In my opinion, an arranger has 50 percent control of the emotional arc of a song. The other 50 percent is controlled by the performers. I've seen many performances where the arrangement and the delivery are out of synch with each other. Either the arrangement isn't able to support the emotional depth of the delivery, or the singers are not performing the arrangement to its emotional potential. When the arrangement and performance are

in complete synchronicity with each other, telling the same story, that's when the magic happens. This is why I like to coach and/or create learning tracks for my arrangements whenever possible.

RD: Ultimately, the performance creates the emotion, but the arranger has a lot to do with setting the group up to succeed or fail. This happens at both a technical and an artistic level. The arrangement has to be idiomatically written to the point that it won't hinder the performers' ability to communicate (i.e., allows for good breathing, doesn't have a lot of awkward voice leading, etc.). Ideally, it also needs to optimally align the core message of the song with an interpretation that the singers can understand and sell with their performance. If the arranger's vision for the song doesn't mesh well with the source material, or if the group doesn't understand the vision, it can get really hairy.

The other thing that I think is really important in crafting emotion in an arrangement is pacing—in other words, the rate and intensity with which the arrangement re-engages the audience. I have a lesson that I include in a lot of my arranging classes where I pull up a chart of the story beats of *Star Wars* and compare it to the moments that happen in the Duke Pitchforks' arrangement of "Hallelujah." The rate at which new ideas are introduced in the arrangement, and the ways in which those ideas intensify and escalate, closely match the way the plot of the movie unfolds—constantly renewing the audience's focus and taking them on a real journey. When this is done well in music, as in film, it's captivating. Pacing in an arrangement has a lot to do with why moments land (or don't), and whether the audience feels moved by a piece of music or not.

DS: All sound, including music, is a matter of four elements: pitch (which with other pitches becomes melody and harmony), duration (which with silence becomes rhythm), loudness (dynamics), and timbre. Are any of these more important in creating an emotional arrangement?

RD: I think they're all equally important. Some of them are probably more easily articulated by an audience (the subtleties of pitch and loudness are probably more instantly recognized by untrained ears than duration and timbre), but all of them are useful tools in creating a mood for your audience.

BB: It's really hard to pick, since they're all so important, but I'd say timbre is the most essential to creating an emotional arrangement. Timbre and tone are how we feel things in music. It's the difference between strong and vulnerable, passionate and indifferent, lovesick and lustful. All these subtle colors are created by way of vocal timbre, in conjunction with body language, facial expression, volume, inflection, etc. But for me, at the heart of it all is timbre.

RD: I think that's a solid point. Pitch and duration (which I'm interpreting as whether something is in tune and whether it grooves) are very important insofar as they need to be done well to not *distract* an audience from the emotional content. Pitch can also create emotional nuances—a little flatness here or a little sharpness there communicates something. Same with duration—little groove changes can add up to big style shifts. Still, timbre definitely carries the most emotional information . . . along with loudness, which I guess may be considered to be the amount of timbre your ears are being sent? *(laughs)*

DS: Beyond making it easier, do you arrange differently for a young group as opposed to old? New as opposed to experienced?

RD: Not really, but I might coach them through it differently. Especially in the case of young singers, I've seen clinicians take for granted that the life experience of an 18-year-old is different from the life experience of a 25-year-old, which is of course different from the life experience of a 50-year-old. Sometimes you can approach a teenager and tell them to "sing this like you're in love," and they'll get it. Sometimes you have to speak more viscerally and universally: "Sing this like the color blue," "Sing this like you're lifting a heavy rock," etc.

BB: Beyond the obvious skill level differences, I don't approach the arrangements any differently. Even my more complex jazz arrangements still follow the same principles I apply to a beginner high school arrangement:

1. **Singability.** This means I'm creating lines that make sense by themselves and are memorable, easy to commit to memory. These lines also have good voice leading, using awkward jumps only when absolutely necessary. If a line sounds good and melodic all by itself, it passes the test. Also, I generally avoid extraneous or hard-to-remember alterations to the repeated sections.

2. **Chord voicings for success.** There are certain intervals and voicings that are easy to sing, easy to tune—generally a home run. Range-wise, I generally keep chords in an

      easy-to-medium range for all, pushing people to their limits only when I know the group is capable of it.

3. **Simplicity overall.** I have seen too many unwieldy arrangements fail in practice, when they are great in theory. After a while, you start to realize the right kind of challenges to give singers. It's very different from what you would give instrumentalists.

4. **Units.** A unit is a grouping of parts that sing the same rhythms and lyrics or syllables together. This could be a gospel trio harmonizing together or a group of three or four singers doing a "guitar" part. In my arrangements, I am very clear and organized with my units. This allows for a very distinct, crisp sound in the background parts.

RD: Obviously, everyone is different, but I think you have to know your audience when it comes to how you're talking to a group about the ideas in your arrangement. On a basic level, though, I try to bake the emotions I want into the arrangement as best I can, regardless of the age or experience of the group it's for.

DS: What specific choices or techniques do you use to imprint greater emotional impact into your arrangements?

RD: I talked about pacing as part of my answer to one of the last questions—that's a huge part of it. As Ben said, tone color is big as well. Vowels and their volume play an important role in how a moment reads. Soft "oo" may evoke vulnerability, loud "ah" anger, etc. Chord voicing can reinforce those decisions, too. Low, closed voicings tend to support more powerful moments, while higher, less stable inversions tend to trigger softer emotions.

BB: One tool I love to employ that's often overlooked is the use of breath. Breathing is of course integral to life, and being that it is involuntary it is also one of our basest and truest forms of expression. There are so many ways to express ourselves through breath without saying a word—sighing, panting, grunting, hyperventilating, relaxed exhaling, etc. The way we breathe is incredibly telling of our emotional state, and our breathing can be aggressive, calm, sensual, nervous, excited, sad, etc. In my arrangements and coaching, I call attention to the use of breath in three key ways:

1. **Before.** The way singers breathe before their entrance can set up the emotional tone with which they'll deliver

the phrase. It could be a long and deep, relaxed breath, or maybe it's a short and jagged catch-breath, which will sound decidedly more urgent and desperate.

2. **During.** The degree of breathiness in a singer's tone is a huge emotional tool to use. Often times, a breathy sound while singing can be used to create a sense of vulnerability and uncertainty. A fuller tone usually sounds strong and confident.

3. **After.** The way singers release a note is also a huge opportunity for emotional expression. You could fall off the note, use a hard stop, or use the breath to release a note, letting it dissolve sensitively. The Nor'easters have a name for this breathy release—they call it "sex breath"—however, I think it can be used to convey much more than just sensuality.

RD: Texture and layering contribute as well—perhaps mostly perceived as how "busy" something is. Typically, the more rhythmically active a moment is, the more an audience will perceive it as "moving forward," which often best supports extroverted emotions (anger, joy, fear). Conversely, less movement can really support more introverted emotional moments—not just because there's less forward propulsion, but also because the lack of bells and whistles tends to put more focus on the lead's lyrics and their meaning.

This is all a pretty big oversimplification, of course—a lot of this is all very dependent on specific moments in specific songs—but those are some things I keep in mind.

DS: What advice do you have for singers who are approaching your arrangements for the first time?

RD: First, please don't take what's on the page so literally. In a choir, things often have to be sung at "face value" so that they can be unified (perhaps "doo" is nice and round, with a sharp attack). In an a cappella group (which tends to be smaller, with sometimes as few as one on a part), things can relax and more individual personality and style can enter into the sound. These days, whenever I can, I'll include a vocal demo of the arrangement along with the score to guide the group's interpretation. It's really the only reliable way to make sure they know what I was thinking.

Second, think about the impact you want the song to have on your audience. I arrange with that impact in mind as well, and singing with an awareness of where the big moments are will add

so much to the performance. When I workshop groups on my arrangements, this is probably the thing I focus on most often.
BB: Sing soulfully yet accurately. Observe all note values and rests; I am very deliberate about those. Have fun with it. Show me some sass!

DS: What advice do you have for young arrangers?
RD: Every single musical experience you have is an opportunity to add something to your "arranging toolbox." Watch other people's work with the same focus with which you watch your own—what would you have done differently? The same? How did the audience react to what they saw? What made them react that way? Etc. Soak up that information and incorporate it into your work.

Ask questions, and be careful about putting anyone's work on a pedestal. If your goal is to be as good as your favorite arranger, and you only work toward that goal, you may never know if you could have been even better . . . or at least have developed your own unique voice.

Every now and then, turn off your critical ears and try to enjoy music free of judgment. It's going to help keep you from burning out and give you a lot more longevity.
BB: Get your musical head out of the a cappella bubble. The a cappella community is fantastic in so many ways, but it can be musically insular. There are so many musical inspirations to be had outside of the bubble. Find them and you can bring something truly new and different to your a cappella arranging.

Make your arrangements fun to sing and relatively simple. If you write something that's extremely difficult and not natural to sing, it could take them out of the moment and into their heads. The best way to ensure a good performance is to be sure that your singers can stay emotionally engaged the whole time.

Roger Emerson and Mac Huff

If you sang music in school, it's pretty much guaranteed that you sang arrangements by Roger and Mac. As the backbone of the Hal Leonard choral arranging department they are responsible for countless arrangements each year, at all levels, for traditional choirs, show choirs, a cappella groups . . . you name it. Roger started out in a rock band, despite his mother's vocal jazz group and his brother's jazz band. Within three years of publishing his first arrangement as an elementary school music teacher, he was making more from his arrangements than from teaching, so he became a full-time arranger and has remained so for the past 35 years. Mac started piano at a young age, with a well-known barbershop arranger and coach for a father. He first tried arranging on a dare from his high school choral teacher; two years later he was arranging the entire show for the Wisconsin Singers show choir, and he has never looked back. With 1700 charts in print, Mac likes to joke that he's "paid by the pound." Both are very popular clinicians as well as arrangers, workshopping groups around the U.S. each year.

DEKE SHARON: You both arrange both a cappella and vocal harmony with instruments in a variety of styles for a variety of levels. Do you find any differences in the way you represent emotion when arranging for different levels of singer, styles of music, or a cappella vs. harmony with instruments?

ROGER EMERSON: Quite frankly, I rarely have thought about the way that I impart emotion into any chart that I have ever arranged. I *do* like to have an arrangement grow and take both the listener and the audience on an aural journey. I have been fortunate to write for all levels of ensembles from elementary to senior citizen, accompanied and a cappella, and I always adhere to the "do no harm" philosophy. Joking aside, pick good tunes and try to make sure that the arrangement does justice to the tune.

As I was thinking about some of my favorites, they would have to be those where I really stretched out from the original, as in "Over the Rainbow," which uses quartal harmony in the opening measures. I'm sure that evokes an "emotion" in the singer and listener, good, bad, or indifferent.

Most of the time, however, I want to make sure that the vocal lines "go where they are supposed to go." What a singer wants to sing and will naturally gravitate to is a paramount consideration.

THE HEART OF VOCAL HARMONY

I have come to the conclusion that many very cool harmonies
to listen to are not necessarily easy to sing. Instrumentalists are
almost unlimited when it comes to unique leaps (unless you are
playing French horn), but it is precisely those leaps that make some
chords come alive.

MAC HUFF: I guess I always come to an arrangement with an emotional point of view. I try to hear the finished product before I
begin to write. I work from the outside in. I begin with the lyric
and how all the musical tools we have at our disposal serve to
make the poetry and content of the lyric come alive. This gets
more challenging as I write for younger singers, as I simply have
fewer choices. In the final analysis, inspired musical direction and
a well-rehearsed group of singers hold the key to expressing emotion in an arrangement.

DS: What are some of the specific techniques you use when arranging a happy song? A sad song? An angry or fearful song?
RE: I'm not sure that I ever ask myself, "Is this a happy song or a
sad song," but rather, "What textures do I want to use?" Realize
that if the arrangement is a current pop hit, the goal for me is to
try and recreate the sound and use the voices and instruments
at my disposal for that purpose. A huge challenge is the extreme
range that so many tenors now have, which I will often double
with altos just to be safe.
MH: As an arranger coming from an emotional point of view, I
make many choices that might affect the successful performance of
a piece. Choice of key, vocal texture and orchestration, instrumental choices, building of a rhythm section groove . . . the list goes
on and on. A few examples: Choosing a key is more than studying
the vocal tessitura and finding a key that best fits the voice. All
keys have different timbres. A rich lullaby is better in E-flat than
E major. However, a lot of grooved pop songs are better in a sharp
key. If the song is angry or dramatic, I might choose a key that is
slightly higher so that a singer is forced to use more of his or her
upper range, creating more tension and drama. Instrumentation
and timbre choices can affect the emotional outcome of a piece.
If I'm arranging a bouncy Jason Mraz piece, I might use ukulele
instead of guitar, giving it a lighter, more happy-go-lucky feel. To
augment that choice, I would keep the vocal textures more thin
and transparent.

DS: Are there any choices you make to ensure that the background parts remain focused and engaged throughout the song?

RE: When you ask about keeping background parts engaging, I have to admit that my hat is off to vocal percussionists who often have to maintain a fairly static part. I'm also not a big fan (from an arranging standpoint) of just a solo that is accompanied by vocals that are imitating a piano part. Although I have used this technique for a section of a piece, I think it becomes boring for both the audience and the singers. One of the aspects of my current two favorite a cappella ensembles, Pentatonix and Groove for Thought, is that the melody often weaves between parts so that both singer and audience get a change of engagement and timbre. Very fine arranging and singing.

MH: One way to keep background vocals engaged is creative, interesting voice leading. I always tell part singers to sing their line as if it were the melody. In the end, all parts in polyphony need to be approached with the same vocal line and musical phrasing as the lead singer. In addition, as Roger said, moving the melody around is also a great technique to keep things interesting and focused.

DS: What advice do you have for young arrangers when it comes to arranging in an emotionally effective way?

RE: My advice to young arrangers is simple: *do it!* There is no substitute for jumping in and creating, trying it out, using your ears, rewriting, etc. Every situation and every ensemble is different, so it is hard to dictate hard and fast rules, but there are some basic considerations. Is this arrangement only for the talents of the group that you are currently writing for, or do you want it to extend to a broader singing audience? If so, it is better to keep the arranging practical, voice leading logical, ranges reasonable, harmonies not too far out.

MH: Roger's advice is fantastic and important. I guess I would add the following: Come to every arrangement with a point of view. Don't be afraid to write and rewrite. If you are writing for your own group, then you're involved in the whole process, from creation to recreation. If something isn't working, then revisit the arrangement. Music software allows us to easily do this. Keep growing as a musician. Surround yourself with quality people and you will go far.

DIRECTORS

Not everyone enters school or the workplace knowing they want to be a choral director, yet along the way some discover that it is their calling. There is something incredibly powerful and compelling in the act of teaching the next generation the art of vocal harmony, or working with a choir of amateur singers whose greatest joys each week come from their time in your group. No one journey is typical, no two groups the same, yet there are universal lessons and insights that apply to all vocal groups, regardless of age or level.

Kathleen Hansen and Mo Field

When you think of Sweet Adelines, you likely think of old songs, barbershop harmonies, sequins, and jazz hands, but not sincere emotional delivery. Kathleen and Mo are two shining stars in the Sweet Adeline community who are bringing an honesty and intensity to every choir they work with, and changing the game throughout the community.

DEKE SHARON: You both direct and coach groups of 100, sometimes 200 or more singers. How do you get all of these people understanding and expressing as a unit when it's impossible for them all to express their own version of the lyrics or otherwise participate in a discussion?

KATHLEEN HANSEN: As a director I feel a great deal of responsibility to create a safe space for singers to tap into emotions they may not otherwise express. Our singers have rich emotional lives that sometimes need to be awakened to find release. To unify the emotional approach, sometimes we have to do a lot of digging to find common ground.

Once in a while, there is a topic that some people just don't identify with. When that happens, we practice stepping into a character. Frequently we'll write a story line: what happened before or after the song takes place? How old is this character? Where *exactly* are they? What is the weather like, what are they wearing, how old are they, what triumphs and tragedies have they experienced in life? We want to tap into people's authentic emotions, but sometimes they need to tell someone else's story to fully accept the character.

DS: I have coined an expression, "riser disease," which is the affliction that strikes singers on risers who think that their face, in a sea of faces, just doesn't matter; no one could be looking at them, so they don't emote. How do you keep every singer feeling engaged and essential to the overall performance?

KH: Ah yes. Riser disease. One advantage we have is that some of our performances are broadcast on a giant screen, so the prospect of having a camera in your face helps a bit. Two main thoughts come to mind:

1. If all of the singers are emotionally and wholly invested in the performance, they're likely going to be "on." That being said, some people emote more naturally than others, so every now and then we have to break it down technically before heading back to the emotional side. We don't always realize we have permanently furrowed eyebrows or tend to close our eyes for long stretches of time when we get into the moment. I like to show videos to my singers—both of other groups that are successful and of our own performances. Invariably, the most common comment is, "I thought I was doing more!"
2. Imagine a lit-up sign in Las Vegas. If you're looking at a Las Vegas–style sign, which bulbs do you notice? The ones that are out or flickering.

MO FIELD: I think of riser disease as either "bunny in the headlights" or "resting bitch face." The thing is this: it really doesn't matter what your face "does" or how you contort it for variety—what people react to is the shining eyes. No glow, no go.

I have seen awesome performers deliver incredibly intricate visual performances, displaying an outstanding array of what they think they are supposed to look like, and it simply comes off as "performing monkeys" or rehearsed emotion. Audiences are far more savvy than we give them credit for, and I insist that they can clock when we are up there for self-interest, and when we are sincerely up there for them and ourselves.

The most rewarding experiences come from practicing "being at play" with that member of the group that can't make it to the rehearsals: the audience. This sort of abandon is not something you wait to turn on; it is a conceptual way of experiencing the joy music gives others, which reflects back to you, the performer.

Being a performer is a position of being of service to another: any set of eyes, ears, a heart. Out there in the audience is at least one person who is right in it with you, all the way, whether you, the performer, can see them or not. I encourage my group and the group's coach to make sure they are being accessible, for you never know who out there in the dark abyss is hanging on your every nuance; you never know who is letting your music and expression heal them.

DS: The barbershop genre is based on a harmonic structure and repertoire from roughly 100 years ago. How do you marry modern technique and emotions with lyrics and traditions from long ago? Are they ever at odds?

MF: A good song is a good song. As a songwriter, I have spent many a night pacing the floor, trying to find that line that encapsulates all the humanity in the prose that is possible, in a way that is a quick grasp for as many people as possible. I suspect that the lyrical poetry of some of the genre's more dated material was also written by a poet who stayed up nights in order to boil the substance of complex human experience down to a digestible nugget for the listener. So I look at lyrics, no matter how dated, in this way—as poetry—and search for the contemporary substrate and meaning inside them, the common denominator, the base human emotion.

Luckily, this is accented by the rise and fall of a melody, and padded by the luscious chords. Add to this the variety of textures available to a singer. The variables at our disposal are far-reaching and especially fascinating to musicians in this genre who are interested in bringing their personal organic expression and mindfulness to the craft, with abandon and an inquisitive nature. All art should reflect life. If not, it is cheating art.

What I consider is that we sing music. It is our imperative to find out, as musicians, all that we can make of it: to know that we are, as performers, but one piece of a creative puzzle, in search of the most exquisite delivery of all the lyric, melody, and arrangement intend, to find the depth in each piece and bring it forward for human consumption. When I think this way, the interpretation of songs becomes a contemporary evolution, regardless of song style, genre, date stamp.

Whether performing Wagner, Aerosmith, Sinatra, contemporary a cappella, or barbershop, it should rock your soul, or you aren't doing it right.

KH: I've only been barbershopping since 1999. Even in that time I've seen a huge shift that has paralleled a lot happening in the choral and pop music worlds. From a technical standpoint, emphasis on particular breathing techniques or approaches to vowels, mouth shape, consonants changes quickly. Think about the airy-voiced, R-less pop vocal style of the 1980s versus the fast vibrato of earlier decades. It's amazing to hear a song written in the early 1900s, arranged in the '70s, then rearranged today. The harmonies hold up well, and I think they're cleaner now than ever before. At some point you need to make a decision: are you performing as a period ensemble or a modern ensemble? I'd say most audiences and singers enjoy the latter. That being said, when we reproduce a performance, we're still viewing that through a modern lens of what we think things were like, so it all ties into today.

DS: Sweet Adelines are known for sequins and big hand gestures, which strike many as antiquated and hammy. How do you reconcile these traditions and instincts with the desire to create honest, intimate moments?

KH: Ay yi yi . . . make it stop! That being said, every genre tends to develop its own vocabulary. Head banging to hard rock, anyone? Performances within a genre tend to eventually become caricatures of themselves.

I think a little bit of information is dangerous—if you say to a beginning actor, "Never turn your back to the audience," they'll produce a disingenuous performance as they awkwardly struggle to figure out how to talk to the person behind them. If you say to a singer, "Here, this gesture shows excitement, energy, emotion," then that will become part of the visual vocabulary.

You see this in politics: stop here, gesture to audience, pound podium. You see it in gymnastics: flick head here to show you nailed the move. Cheerleading: choreographed winking . . . the list goes on. From symphonic conductors to street performers,

THE HEART OF VOCAL HARMONY

we pick up on visual vernacular. We just need to be aware of the difference between authentic communication and overacted, cheeseball antics.

MF: Many groups are full of people who follow trends. Trends are set up by perceived success. If one group does it and gets rewarded, it will appeal to other groups. Training a chorus to think for themselves and discover their own identity is a journey into discovery of the individual, and a balance of bringing the full individual to the forefront of contribution to the collective expression. But sadly, we tend to parrot what is presented and rewarded. There is very little chance to stretch outside the lines if the group is needing to be affirmed from an external source.

Those groups that do extend themselves beyond stereotype and cliché might well lose the contest, but they will consistently win the audience. Personally, as a director, and within my chorus, we do not reconcile these notions. We have decided to do our own thing, and actually reimagine how we can play with the organization's largely dated concepts in order to create room for change.

I am reminded of the genius of Mozart—whilst trying to compose in a time when music theory dictated what was "allowed" and not allowed, what made him a genius was that he didn't break the rules, nor did he play by them—he went and found the area that had not been regulated and started exploring. Barbershop is like this for me. It is so much more than is currently allowable, and going to play in those nether regions is actually quite interesting.

DS: It's not uncommon to have a Sweet Adeline chorus have members that span 60 years in age, a wide variety of backgrounds, with both professional and new singers side by side. How do you overcome such vast differences in age, experience, and ability in your choirs? Are there ever problems you can't reconcile?

KH: It is better to embrace than to overcome. It creates frustration when we don't all come from the same background, but if you can develop a culture in which everyone can respect and learn from each other's experiences, and learn to effectively communicate, it becomes one of our strengths rather than a weakness. There's no magic potion—it takes a deliberate effort to sculpt this culture.

MF: Whilst we love to say, "Everyone is welcome" and boast diversity, I am going to go on record and say this: when it comes to ageism, and socio-economic diversity, the barbershop world is advanced indeed! You can stand in a room of peers, feeling as absolute equals, and not even consider age as a status issue in any way. In this, these communities operate on a fantastic basis of matrix rather than hierarchy.

However, when it comes to cultural competence, this is not necessarily the case. Barbershop communities tend to be fairly insular. Barbershop was an African American expression originally, gentrified and codified by a largely white and exclusive group. Whilst I would love to say that this is no longer the case, I do see that more millennials are attracted who have a broader cultural background, but I fear this is an accident of sorts.

The continued use of music from minstrelsy, or music depicting the grandeur of the pre–civil rights South, is rampant and ill-researched by the singer. It is akin to the "big hair and sequins" discussion: if it wins, people think it's okay, and sadly, our "approves of suitable contest material" committee has not had the chance to review the ideas of cultural competence that reflect an inclusive vision for all. Not all old or regional songs are offensive, but a great many people do not do their due diligence when it comes to repertoire selection, and frankly, much of what we tend to sing is flat-out offensive to nonwhite, non-Christian cultures.

Barbershop, as a corporate identity and larger community, for some reason, is largely America-centric, often Christian expressive, white, hetero, and cis normative. Much education is needed in this area. However, on a one-on-one basis, some of the most welcoming people you could ever meet.

Lisa Forkish

Few people have put their stamp on contemporary a cappella as compellingly as Lisa Forkish, and she's done it more than once. As music director of Divisi, she changed the sound of women's collegiate a cappella, marching her new group all the way to the ICCA finals at Lincoln Center, a tale immortalized in the book and then the movie *Pitch Perfect*. Then she started a group at Oakland School for the Arts and created Vocal Rush, who have won the International Championship of High School A Cappella (ICHSA) finals three times, once with only her women when none of the guys in her group could make the trip. Vocal Rush also appeared on *The Sing-Off* and made it all the way to the finals, knocking out many professional groups as they inspired high schoolers around the nation to sing professional a cappella regardless of their age. More than once when working with high schoolers I have asked myself, "WWLD? What would Lisa do?"

DEKE SHARON: What made you want to be a director?
LISA FORKISH: I don't recall thinking, "I want to be a director." As a senior in high school, I got into the University of Oregon's all-female group Divisi (they needed female basses, so they let me join as a high school student, provided I took a class on campus), and I caught the a cappella bug. I was elected to be Divisi's music director in my second year when I was only a college freshman and served for three years. I learned a lot about how to lead, how to manage different personalities, how to command a room full of singers. With a small group, you can get tight with the other singers in ways that enhance the music and take your performance to new heights. We were connected on and off stage, and I learned a great deal about the importance of emotional connection, not just to the song you are singing, but to the singers who stand on either side of you. I've taken those lessons with me into my professional directing career, and I believe it has served my students, perhaps even more than the musical training itself.

DS: What makes a good director? How do you approach directing?
LF: I'm good at it because I love it. I think that's important to note. If you want to be a great director but you don't love the work all that much, it's going to be tough to get there. One of the things I love about being a vocal director is that every day is different. You're dealing with people (and in my case, young, hormonal

people), and I kind of love the challenge of each day having its own shape and form, its own unique beautiful moments of music making, its own sometimes quiet moments of personal transformation (for me and the students!). And of course, I love making music, and as a director I get to do that every day. Even though I'm not singing in the group, I am still making music. Being a director is like being in the driver's seat of a car full of really passionate and excited people who don't really know where they want to go—or maybe they do and they disagree. Much of the job is getting everyone to want to travel to the same place, and then getting them there, all the while enjoying the journey itself.

I mostly direct with my gut. I'm a sensitive person with a natural inclination toward compassion, empathy, vulnerability, and connection. Teaching from this place doesn't mean it's all touchy-feely or that we sit and talk about our feelings every day; it just means that when we access empathy and vulnerability from the get-go, we can get to an authentic vocal performance early on. It's not something you have to work up to. When you have vulnerability, you have courage. The two go hand in hand. And especially as the person in a position of power, by making myself vulnerable, compassionate, open, I allow that space for my singers. It is these qualities that lead me and are the driving force behind my directing style and philosophy. In the early years, I think I tried to squash that part of myself because I didn't see it in other directors and educators, so I assumed it was "wrong." More recently, though, I've owned those qualities as my strengths as a director, and I've also acknowledged that whatever success I've achieved over the years . . . well, I need to give credit where credit is due. Many directors put on a front with their singers. Or get on a power trip. Or bring a lot of ego into the rehearsal. But how can we expect singers to go "leave it all onstage," with an emotionally charged, powerful, genuine, connected performance (which is what we all want to see, and ask to see) without us as directors giving that of ourselves behind the scenes?

DS: When forming Vocal Rush, what was your goal?
LF: The true story behind why I formed Vocal Rush was not the party line at the time. When I announced that I was forming an extracurricular contemporary a cappella group that would rehearse one day a week after school, the party line was that I was forming a group to take to *The Sing-Off* Season Three auditions a

few months later. The real reason? I needed to gain the students' respect. I was a new teacher, a young teacher, hired mid-year to replace a teacher who was burnt out and didn't want to deal with this particular group of students. They felt abandoned by their original director, and of course I was the recipient of all this pain and resentment. I left work every day in tears. They were breaking me down after just a couple of months and I was desperate. I wanted to stay at this job, but I needed to gain rapport with the students. I needed their respect.

My theory was that if I could get even a small group of them to take a chance on a new director, I could show them what I had to offer and we could really get to know each other. Then their changed attitude toward me would seep into the rest of the department and I could start making music with these students instead of pulling teeth every day. It worked. I gained the students' respect. And Vocal Rush became more than just an extracurricular group. We worked it into the daily curriculum, and it became the department's top performing ensemble, not to mention three-time national champions, third place winners on *The Sing-Off*, etc. All in a matter of years. Those weren't my initial goals, but I think any good leader knows that once you reach one goal, you have to set your sights on another, and then another, and then another . . . We've never arrived. We continue to grow year after year, setting new goals all the time.

DS: How and why do you choose songs? How does emotion play a role?
LF: I always consider the message of a song before choosing it. Vocal Rush has never done many of the silly love songs with shallow messages that pervade the pop music world. I just don't think that's what young people should be getting on stage and singing about. We've got bigger fish to fry! I've also found that choosing songs with an important message that students can connect to is a shortcut to some of that vulnerability, connection stuff I talked about earlier. The song is the means. If you're singing about rubbing up against someone on the dance floor, it's going to be hard to get your singers to get emotionally connected, and consequently nearly impossible to get the audience on board.

That's not to say that all the songs we sing are serious. We do fun stuff, too, like "Tightrope," by Janelle Monae, "Upside Down," by Paloma Faith, and "Green Garden," by Laura Mvula—

all upbeat, lighter songs but with a deeper message that singers and audiences can connect to. We don't take ourselves too seriously. We have a lot of fun, and I think our fun is even more fun because we know each other better; we feel comfortable being ourselves. It's about authenticity more than anything else. My students have been saying to me this year, "Ms. Forkish, is that your favorite word or something?" So, yeah, I think I talk about that a lot in my teaching.

DS: How do you run rehearsal; what have you changed over the years?

LF: One thing I've learned over the years is when to give your singers time and space for input. When I directed Divisi I was only 18, and I was directing my peers. I imagine that I allowed a lot of time for other singers to weigh in, but sometimes you end up talking more than singing, and that's a problem. I've learned to give myself permission to take the reins and keep them for a chunk of rehearsal, especially when polishing up a new song, and then allow time later in the rehearsal for students to jump in with their ideas. I strongly believe that students should have a voice in the rehearsal, but what I've cleaned up over the years is the way I structure that.

I also don't take time in rehearsals to teach notes and rhythms. Much like in a professional group, I require my students to learn their music outside of class or rehearsal, and then they are given what we call a "rep check," where they have to sing one on a part and are graded one point per measure. Groups who aren't a part of a school or class don't have this option, but you can still build it in using accountability as the motivator, not the grade. Most times, students are more concerned about being accountable to one another than they are about their grade, anyway. This allows us to get right to the polishing stage of rehearsal—we can talk song meaning, story arc, build, dynamics, color, tone, nuance, delivery, etc. right away. Four months into the year and Vocal Rush has learned over 15 songs. I wish I'd known the magic of this model when I directed Divisi! It's a great way to establish accountability, as I said, as well as strong work ethic, responsibility, time management—and of course the fabulous by-product is hours and hours of freed-up rehearsal time to make music.

DS: How do you create a safe space/environment for emotional singing?

LF: Beyond what I've already said, I lead a team-building retreat every fall where the singers spend a full weekend doing activities related to identity, diversity, group culture, and leadership. The students anticipate it every year, knowing that there is a huge shift after that weekend—the retreat itself establishes group norms and expectations for a safe space and allows the students to open up to each other. That environment then translates into the rehearsal and we can feel safe getting emotional and vulnerable with the music. After you've shared about your identity, connecting to a song feels relatively risk-free. The only challenge then is maintaining that safe space over the course of a year. We usually take time to check in periodically, sometimes just personal check-ins and sometimes group-dynamic check-ins. I also sometimes incorporate team-building activities here and there throughout the year, as well as reminders about group norms.

The newest contributor to the creation of our safe rehearsal space is meditation. This fall, we decided to start every rehearsal with a three- to six-minute guided mindfulness meditation. I always notice a difference on the days we don't do mindfulness; just taking a few minutes to allow the singers to connect to their breath and be with their own thoughts or clear their head starts us off on the right foot. All the singers are ready to give of themselves after having a moment completely to themselves to center and regroup.

DS: How do you deal with emotional crises? Overwhelm during rehearsal?

LF: All of the above. Everything I just mentioned—I use these techniques to deal with challenging group dynamics and emotional crises between members or with an individual. Mindfulness is an *incredible* tool for overwhelm during rehearsal. As the director, it's easy to feed into the overwhelm, lose your cool, and put the blame back on the singers (and of course, I'm guilty of falling victim to this trap). But it's only going to escalate the situation. I would recommend deciding as a group in advance what you will use as a deescalating mechanism—a meditation practice, a song, a warm-up, an inside joke, whatever works—for those moments when it feels like everyone is about to break down.

DS: With so many wins over the years, what have you learned about competing that others should know?

LF: I've learned a lot about competition because Vocal Rush has done a lot of it—and has won most of the competitions they've entered. It's problematic when a group always wins, because then it can easily become about winning and solely about winning. Any good director knows that the best part of taking your group to competition is not the possibility of winning or the win itself, should that be the case. Rather, the best part is the process of preparing for a competition, the striving, the goal itself. Without fail, it always leads to a more excellent version of the group. Except, when it's only about the winning, that can destroy a healthy group dynamic. I would caution directors against giving in to the notion that you prepare for a competition to win. That may sound funny coming from a director of a group that has done a lot of winning, but trust me, I've learned a great deal more from the times Vocal Rush lost than from the times they won. And not about what the students could have done better, but about what I could have done better to steer them in the right direction. Not musically speaking, but in attitude and perspective.

Last year was the most positive competition experience that I've had with Vocal Rush, and it was because they wanted to share their message through song. That was the ultimate goal. They wanted to win, of course, but it wasn't the number one goal. At ICHSA finals last spring, after delivering an emotionally wrought, vulnerable, and powerful version of Sara Bareilles' "Brave," then turning around to reveal the words "#BlackLivesMatter" on their backs, the students came off stage in tears. I was in tears, we were all sobbing and hugging and laughing. And every single singer said, "I don't care what happens now. We did it. It doesn't matter if we win." Hands down, proudest director moment right there. To get your singers to truly deliver and give of themselves onstage and feel completely satisfied having moved and inspired an audience—that is the ultimate win. And I've heard students say that they don't care about winning before. This time, I knew they really meant it, because it was about the performance, the audience connection, and the message of the song. I hope more groups start approaching competitions—and all performances for that matter—from that angle.

J.D. Frizzell

J.D. Frizzell is a force of nature. As the full-time director of Fine Arts and Vocal Music at Briarcrest Christian School in Memphis, Tennessee, J.D. cofounded the A Cappella Education Association, is on the staff at Camp A Cappella, and founded CadenzaOne and The Choir Coach, all while a candidate for the DMA in Choral Conducting degree at the University of Kentucky. Which explains why he was chosen by the board of the Tennessee Music Educators Association as the 2011 Outstanding Young Music Educator. He won the 2007 Intégrales Composition Contest, has dozens of published choral works, and his award-winning high school a cappella ensemble, OneVoice, is a Sony Recording Artist.

DEKE SHARON: What made you want to be a director?

J.D. FRIZZELL: When I went to college, I was studying music, but I did not want to teach or be a director. I wanted to be a composer. I think all young musicians go through this mind-set of, like, "I'm really good at X (with X being any aspect of music in which it's difficult to make money), so I want to do that for a living!" Then reality sets in that the jobs in music are mostly in teaching, not because the other things like composing aren't as worthy and viable, but teaching involves human connection. It involves interacting with people on a day-to-day basis and changing their lives through what you're doing. It makes a huge difference in people's lives, which is why there are so many jobs in teaching and conducting.

DS: You had many music directors over the years. What about their styles and techniques have you wanted to change or improve upon?

JDF: If anything, it would have been the emotional connection to the music. We forget as directors that our students don't have as much experience with this music as we do, and we forget that we need to provide some common ground in terms of emotional and historical context so that we can at least start a dialogue about the emotional connection to the music.

Particularly in choral settings, it is very easy to focus on perfectionism over expression, and that's where I think in general a lot of choral directors may miss the mark, including myself. Directors in general tend to miss the emotional connections to the song, and before even that I think directors miss that they have to teach students about style and the connection between style and emotional honesty.

The emotional connection starts with an understanding of the musical elements that make a listener viscerally feel a given song. Your singers will properly feel it and replicate it when they understand it, and it will start to sound like what they hear on the radio. That's the point at which emotional connection truly becomes a powerful tool. It can happen before that point; it's just much more difficult. If it's not musically great, you're almost forcing the issue emotionally.

DS: What has been the biggest improvement in your directing over the years?

JDF: If I had to pick one thing, it would be the speed of learning music and getting it performance ready. The method that I use now involves students learning their parts on their own and using practice tracks and sheet music, and then we have a practice process by which we take that into a performance-ready mode, typically within a week. They're learning music fast because they can learn the notes quickly on their own and we can get to the emotional connection quickly as a result. It used to take us a month to learn a song, sitting at a piano banging out parts, and by the end of that process people had very little energy with which to approach emotion; we were just ready to move on to another song. That's why I am so against directors banging out notes on the piano for contemporary a cappella, because I feel like it does take away from the ability to connect emotionally.

DS: How and why do you choose songs? How does emotion play a role?

JDF: When we're choosing songs, especially for our albums, we talk a lot during the planning process about what music we could connect to naturally. What styles and artists and songs are on the kids' playlists right now? What do they find themselves listening to and singing along with over and over again? Once we do that, we start to talk about the themes. What are these songs about? Why do you like singing them? And we put the song ideas through a large sieve of different filters. Do we have a soloist or multiple soloists that could really deliver that song stylistically? Is it appropriate for us as a school to be performing? Is it something that would easily work in an a cappella setting? Because I include the singers in the song selection process, they have buy-in to those songs when we actually sing them. I think that's tremendously important.

DS: How does that translate to rehearsal? How do you run rehearsal and prepare a new song?

JDF: When we are rehearsing the songs, when we get to the emotional stage, we go around and ask all of the singers to talk individually about what the song is saying to them or how they connect to it emotionally. And then, once we've told those stories, we try to crowd-source a single emotion that can encapsulate the things that people are saying. If this song could only be about one emotion that most accurately encapsulates the theme, what would that one emotion be? And that gets them thinking more specifically than "sad," "happy," and gets them thinking more along the lines of "angst," "frustration," "overjoyed," "triumph." These emotions are just more specific, which makes the delivery as a group ultimately more impactful.

When we have a new piece, we have sheet music and practice tracks (that the arranger or I will sing). The students meet in the auditorium on stage, we listen through the song once, and then they go and spread out in the auditorium with ear buds and they practice for forty-five minutes. Then we come back together and we sing it once through. It's usually not perfect by any means. Then they will go home and practice. The next day they will come back, I will give them 10 minutes, and then we will start singing it together. At this point in the process, I'm fixing only musical things, usually connecting the parts together, whether it's a complex rhythmic entrance or bell tones at the end of a phrase. Day three involves fixing vowels, phase shape, and dynamics, along with continuing to improve difficult passages.

By day four of rehearsal, we are usually ready to start talking about emotion. I like injecting emotion at that early stage because we've pushed this musical learning process to happen so quickly that there hasn't been too much repeated reading and they aren't too disconnected from that learning process. I think, by it being so quick, that they're still really open to different emotional possibilities and how those might impact the performance. Day four is when we do the emotional process that I described in the previous question. Once we've done that, on day five we are ready to perform. It's not going to be perfect, it's not going to be ready for national choral festivals, but we perform, and we typically do it in front of an audience. We take the students around to a classroom or sing in front of the school for whoever wants to listen. By doing that, we grow substantially and are ready to take that piece to the next level. We're not done with that piece at that point. I will continue to bring it back in small segments over the coming weeks and tweak little sections and continue to make it sound better. But 95 percent of the work on any given piece is done in that initial five-day / one-week period of time.

DS: How do you create a safe space and environment for emotional singing?

JDF: Most of the time we sing with no one in the room, but I welcome guests at any point in the learning process because I want my students to be focused no matter what is going on, and I think that allows them to feel safe regardless of who is there or what they're feeling in their life at the current moment. They're allowed to come into our rehearsal and feel like it's a sanctuary in which they can focus on only what we're doing. That is tremendously important.

Something else that directors need to remember is that we can't bring our own issues into the rehearsal process unless it is a part of the teaching process, something that organically happens when you are talking about a connection to a song. You can't come into a rehearsal, get frustrated, and say, "Guys, I'm having a really bad day. You're going to need to sing really well for me today." That doesn't work. That doesn't create a safe space for the singers, because then instead of making great music and connecting to it emotionally, the motivation is fear: fear of letting down the director, fear of getting in trouble, etc. That is not as powerful as supported self-motivation.

DS: Are there any things to watch out for when discussing emotion in rehearsal? Do you have any techniques that help create a safe space for emotional performance, or help create emotional consistency in every run-through?

JDF: When you are discussing an emotional connection in music, you can't invalidate someone's opinion. By that I mean, you say, "What does the song mean to you?" and maybe someone who's younger and hasn't had as much experience emotionally says something that seems immature. A freshman might say something that a senior will roll their eyes at and be like, "Well, you haven't really had a romantic relationship, so what do you know?" That's really dangerous. I don't let my students discount someone else's feelings.

We forget how real our emotions are when we're young. In fact, sometimes they're more magnified when we're at that developmental stage than when we're adults. Do you remember when you were in middle school and you had that first crush? I remember it was pretty much all I could think about, and every emotion found in that one person was unbelievably intense. I think that is one of the biggest mistakes anyone in the profession of vocal music makes: they assume or they tell young students that their emotions and that their life experiences are sometimes not as valid as adults'. It's just untrue.

Once we have a very open and honest discussion about the lyrics and then tell personal stories relating to those lyrics, we decide on one very specific emotion that best encapsulates the song. I then have each group member think of an event, person, memory, etc. in their own life that makes them feel that emotion. We practice what I call "centering" before we start any song, which is a three- to five-second period of time during which members close their eyes, focus on whatever makes them feel that emotion, then open their eyes. We immediately blow the pitch pipe (if needed) and start the song.

DS: How do you deal with emotional crises? Overwhelm during rehearsal?

JDF: We've had a lot of these: we've lost students tragically, we've lost family members, we've experienced failure and defeat. When these things happen, we put the people first. I am the biggest advocate of anybody I know of singing as much as humanly possible in a rehearsal, but when emotional crises happen, those have to come first; people have to come first. Singers will only be as open as possible with you as a director if they feel like you care about them as a person.

When these things happen to us, we talk about it, we pray about it, we hug, we connect, and we create a bond. We call ourselves a family, and as in any family that translates into the way we treat each other every day and the way that we approach our problems collectively and individually. It's scary as a director to then take those difficult situations and try to connect them emotionally to the rehearsal process. It has to be done in a really careful way, but it can be really powerful if it happens.

I remember when you were working with OneVoice this summer at Camp A Cappella. I didn't even go in there, because I didn't want them thinking about what I would feel or what I was thinking about this master class with you. I wanted them to just be them, and I wanted to see what would happen when you pushed them. And you knew about what had been going on, and the loss that we just had [students killed in a car crash], and it was hard. I know that that process for you and for them was overwhelming, but it produced some of the most authentic and powerful singing that I have ever heard them do. I think that when we can be open and create a safe environment for them to do that, we're not only setting them up for better music-making, we're also preparing them to be more emotionally healthy and open adults.

Joshua Habermann

Joshua is a superstar in the choral music world, with a resume filled with some of America's finest choral ensembles. He got his doctorate at the University of Texas while singing in Conspirare, assistant-conducted the San Francisco Symphony Chorus while building the choral program at San Francisco State University, later headed the choral department at the University of Miami, and now directs two nationally recognized ensembles, the Dallas Symphony Chorus and Santa Fe's Desert Chorale, while sitting on the board of Chorus America. Blending traditional with modern, Western with Eastern, scholastic with professional, his approach to choral singing is wide-ranging, passionate, and engaging.

DEKE SHARON: You speak eight languages and are a very talented athlete and an in-demand educator. Why have you chosen classical choral music as your calling? What do you find uniquely powerful about the form?

JOSHUA HABERMANN: I love choral music because it's the ultimate team sport. Together we can create something that is impossible to accomplish alone. Choral music satisfies a basic human need to belong to something bigger than ourselves, while exposing us to some of the most profound and beautiful words and music ever written. Best of all, we get to perform with and for communities of colleagues and friends.

DS: Many of the pieces of music you conduct are in another language, written in another era for people whose culture and way of life differed from our own. How do you make these pieces relevant and emotionally compelling for both your singers and your audiences?

JH: I think in every piece there's a story. It can be the personal story of the composer or the poet, or possibly of the occasion for which the piece was written. Then we have the text, which our singers must understand and internalize in order to project and recreate the story. Any one of these touchpoints can be a window in—a way to make the music alive and relevant for our performers and the listener. In this way choral music teaches empathy; it creates an awareness of another's story and how it might be reflected in our own.

DS: How do you find working with the Desert Chorale different from the Dallas Symphony Chorus? Are they both equally capable of emotional expression?

JH: Beyond the size of the groups (24 voices in Santa Fe versus 185 in Dallas), there aren't significant differences regarding emotional expression and communication. Because the Symphony Chorus most often performs with the orchestra in a large hall, we do have to work harder to connect individually with audience members because of the physical distance. I often say that people hear what they see, and chamber choirs benefit from being closer to the listener, which facilitates person-to-person connection and communication.

DS: Everyone wants to hear choral music during the holidays, but that's only a twelfth of the year. How do you draw audiences the other eleven months? Moreover, choirs and classical music in general have been seeing diminishing audiences around the U.S., and yet both of your organizations are thriving with audiences that increase each year. What advice can you offer a fellow director of classical choral music?

JH: Sustaining and growing audiences is a constant challenge, but I don't share the negative view of where we are headed. There's no question that recent technological innovations have made it easier to access anything from anywhere, and to a certain extent this has depressed live concert attendance. However, we know from the recent Chorus America survey that there are over 43 million Americans participating in choral music in the United States, so we know the art form isn't going away; in fact, it's growing.

In addition to this, there is no question that live performance is a qualitatively different experience from listening to a recording. Through technology we are increasingly connected, but also isolated in terms of meaningful human contact. Live concerts offer just that connection, not only between performers and audience, but also among the audience members themselves, who form a listening community. The need for connection and community is a basic human impulse, and nothing exemplifies those ideals better than choral music.

The upshot of this is that if we want to maintain and grow our audiences we need to offer them concert experiences that are meaningful and emotionally connected. It's worth noting that there can be meaningful and communicative performance at all age and skill levels. I have attended performances of the highest technical quality that left me less moved than concerts of less technically skilled but more emotionally connected groups. This is not to say that the emotional piece can replace the technical quality that we strive for, but if our art form is to remain relevant, the concert experience has to be more than technically excellent, because that excellence is now available with just a few keystrokes.

DS: You seem to be perpetually looking beyond the standard repertoire: your thesis was on Finnish composer Einojuhani Rautavaara, and your sabbatical on the choral music of the Pacific Rim. What compels you to continue to search for new and obscure choral works and traditions?

JH: Programming concerts is one of the most important aspects of a choir director's job. Unlike our orchestral colleagues, whose concerts most often consist of larger works (overtures, concertos, symphonies), our art form is largely made up of shorter pieces. The challenge, then, is to create a meaningful and memorable concert experience that is more than what a friend of mine calls "chicken-soup programming," in which you throw together a bunch of loosely related pieces and call it a concert.

Knowing the breadth and depth of the literature that is out there is a huge part of creating a concert that has a flow and reso-nates with both performers and audience. Again, with the excep-tion of the larger works (the great requiems, *Carmina Burana*, etc.), there are no popular hits in the choral canon. In many ways, this is freeing, as choral ensembles are not confined by a "museum" of pieces in the same way as many orchestras. We are free to explore the very rich and varied repertoire from around the world. Know-ing as much of that repertoire as possible is a huge aid in creating interesting concert experiences.

Picking up again on the subject of empathy, I would add that vocal music, which is common to all human cultures, is also an excellent conduit to explore traditions outside our own. Experienc-ing a wide variety of music brings us into meaningful contact with other cultural traditions. Though the languages may be unfamiliar, the themes and stories we humans sing are universal.

DS: What tips and techniques have you learned from other forms and traditions of vocal music that you've brought to your cho-ruses?

JH: Some of my colleagues in the classical world lament the rise of pop music and what they perceive as the lowering of standards in music education. While I understand that point of view, I think there are things that choruses, and classical choruses in particular, can and should learn from other traditions. Anyone who attends a concert by a great pop a cappella group can appreciate the communication and emotional impact that music offers. I believe the best performers are those in any genre whose authenticity helps to break down barriers between people and reveal the energy that connects us. Pop and folk performers are doing a better job of this than classical groups, and we need to learn from them.

The last thing I would add is the importance of choosing great music, and by great music I don't necessarily mean classical music. I mean in whatever genre you are doing, choose the very highest quality. If it's a jazz tune, then choose a great jazz tune, a great pop tune, a great folk tune, etc. Our singers and audiences know quality when they hear it, even children. If we want them to have and share an emotional connection with the music, then we should be very sure that the music we choose is inspiring. If we are passionate about the music, our audiences will feel that and respond.

Bruce Rogers

In every field, there are superstars well known by their colleagues but unknown to the outside world. Bruce is such an individual, with a sterling reputation in classical choral as well as vocal jazz circles. He has many awards and has conducted in many different countries, but you may know him best as Pentatonix bass Avi Kaplan's former choral director.

DEKE SHARON: How did your early days of acting and rock 'n' roll music educate you, and do they inform your musical choices now?
BRUCE ROGERS: Both of the above activities from my youth have strongly influenced my classical choirs as well as my vocal jazz groups. I realized when I first started teaching at the middle school and high school levels that I needed to "hook" them with quality popular music, jazz, and Broadway show tunes so I could get them into my classroom, where I could then teach them the joys of classical music and proper vocal technique.

When I was a young conductor in the 1980s, I would attend professional choral and orchestral concerts throughout southern California. All the groups had incredible voices and performed very challenging music, performing them in a very standard way—standing on risers, holding music folders, with no facial expressions or movement. I'd look around at the audience, and it was always filled with elderly men and women. I began to realize that if classical music didn't find a way to appeal to the younger generation, these types of choirs would be in trouble when their audience members eventually passed away. I would also attend choral conventions at the state level and at the national level, where again I witnessed incredible high school and university choirs, with incredible voices, that left me incredibly cold. There was no connection between the singers and the audience, and even if a choir was outstanding, many of the audience members would be flipping through their programs while the choir was singing. My musical goal in life became that I wanted the entire audience, from the music aficionados to Uncle Joe who was dragged to the concert because his niece was performing, to feel as if they were part of the performance.

It is important to note that staging, movement, and facial expression will never make up for poor singing. Visual and musical effectiveness must go hand in hand. I always choose incredibly challenging music for my choirs, and they must first learn to perform each piece with their focus directed on intonation, diction, phrasing, dynamics, etc. before they ever begin to use staging and movement. The staging and expression then help the students take ownership of the song and the text, which in turn is then relayed to the audience, capturing each audience member in a web of emotion of what the text is truly trying to say and what the composer is trying to relate.

DS: You have created a world-class multi-style choral program at a community college, where you have many students for only a year or two, less campus life than a four-year college, and lots of students who are busy working full time or returning to college after a break. All of this would apparently make it impossible to create a great, consistent program. On behalf of all the directors out there who are working in less than ideal conditions, how do you do it?

BR: First off, I'm afraid there is no magic formula. It is up to each individual conductor/teacher to discover what works best for them by using their personal teaching strengths and by making each rehearsal something very special. I will tell you that everyone wants to be part of something that is successful. So that is why I felt it was extremely important when I began at Mt. San Antonio College to immediately build at least one choir that could sing difficult music with excellent musicianship skills and technique. I also wanted that choir to perform all different styles of music, to appeal to the variety of tastes of the student body. I needed a choir that could perform for potential incoming students that would make them want to attend a two-year college over a four-year university. Without singers in your rehearsal room, there really isn't much you can do to build a program. So this needs to be your first focus: recruiting.

Secondly, it became very evident that the program needed to be about the students . . . not about me. Yes, it is important to have the students want to sing well because they like you and respect you as a person and a director, but it is even more important that they each take ownership in the program and take accountability for themselves. I found it incredibly valuable to appoint student leaders for the group and then to have them keep their fellow singers accountable for learning their music, turning in paperwork on time, etc. I discovered that not wanting to let their friends down was more important to them than their grade—which meant it became very important to make sure that they all became close friends. We go on a choral retreat at the beginning of each year and spend most of the weekend just getting to know each other. We also go on a tour each year, which is always a wonderful bonding experience. My student leaders set up choir parties and choir hikes and choir movie get-togethers, etc. All of these events make them feel like a family, which in turn helps them to take ownership in the program, because it's not just about the music. We always talk about the responsibility we have to each other and to our audiences to make the best music possible—not for the sake of the music, but for the sake of the experience. Each concert should be an event, not just a bunch of songs. Each rehearsal should also be an experience not to be missed—not just pounding notes and learning rhythms.

Once these two issues were addressed, everything else just came together. The more our choirs succeeded, the more they wanted to push themselves to be better. Each incoming student immediately feels the love in the group and also feels the pressure, or should I say the challenge, to perform at least as well as last year's group. That pressure never, ever comes from me. The students challenge themselves because they have seen how the audiences react to their concerts and that any performance could possibly change someone's life; so they push themselves to strive for excellence for those reasons alone. As a director, you are bound for failure if you put too much pressure on your students and only talk about the performance in a way that makes it seem like the number one priority of the concert is to impress your audience.

Traditions and discipline are also a huge part in building a successful choral program. Students want and need discipline and structure in their lives, especially at a community college. They also love to be part of a tradition. Most of my incoming students want to sing in our program because of an emotional experience they had in high school when they heard our choirs perform. Once they make one of our groups, they want to give someone else that same experience. We have a tremendous alumni base who continuously come in just to visit, and they always tell my current singers how much they miss being part of the group. They know that they are now part of the extended family, and the current students know that they will someday be part of that extended family and that it will last for a lifetime.

DS: You are one of the few directors in the world who is equally fluent with classical, pop, and jazz idioms. Do you find there are any inherent differences between them? Are there differences in the ways you approach them?

BR: There are definitely differences and similarities in each genre of music. First off, vocal technique should always be everyone's main focus and should be the same for every type of music. Proper breath support and vocal technique should not vary whether you are performing classical, jazz, musical theater, or gospel music. Secondly, every kind of vocal music should express the text in a way that lets the audience receive it as the composer intended. We are singers, not an orchestra or a band (unless you're performing a jazz piece with all scat syllables), so we need to be sure to make the text our number one priority. Learning the correct notes and rhythms and performing a song with outstanding musicality is also important in every type of music.

The differences are found in *stylizing* the music. Each genre of music has a different style and performance practice. Just as performing a piece by Bach should obviously be stylized differently than if you perform a piece by Brahms, performing a vocal jazz piece should also be quite different than performing a Broadway show tune. When we attended college, we studied performance practice for classical music, but probably not for other styles of music (which includes multicultural music). It is important that, as a director, you listen to a plethora of music in the style you want your choir to perform, as well as doing research, before you begin teaching that style to your choir. If you don't want to do the research, you shouldn't perform the music! Be respectful of all music genres that you wish to perform and know what you are doing before you step into a rehearsal.

Additional differences between performing most classical music pieces and other musical styles range from the role of the conductor, the number of singers in your group, and the amount of vibrato in the tone to dealing with sound equipment, microphone technique, a rhythm section, choreography, improvisation techniques, even different music vocabulary.

DS: When it comes to emotional singing, what do these different styles have to learn from each other?

BR: I approach every musical style in the same way. Every type of music should be expressive and text driven, and should connect with the audience. I guess one could say that musical theater is the one genre of music that seems to encompass all of those qualities, but I believe that we can add some "musical theater" elements to our classical, pop, and jazz songs. As I mentioned earlier, you must be careful to do everything tastefully and not as a gimmick. Proper singing and style must always be your first priority; then decide what you can do to enhance the musical experience for the audience or express the text in an appropriate way.

DS: You are also known for your powerful staging choices, integrating the physical with the vocal. What are your guiding principles when adding movement, and how can movement accentuate emotion?

BR: I will attempt to list my priorities with my thoughts concerning staging:

1. Your first priority should be to perform every song with choral integrity and appropriate vocal technique.
2. Any staging that you decide to do must make sense with the text and the style of music you are performing. Never stage for show; stage a piece to enhance the experience.
3. Make sure, if you are staging multicultural music, that you have done your research and that the movements you are adding are appropriate to the cultural style. It can be offensive if you perform movements that would never be done in that particular culture.
4. Don't over-stage a piece to the point where it is difficult to tell what is actually going on in the music or with the text.
5. Be careful not to use choreography or staging that will inhibit the singers' use of proper vocal technique.
6. Just changing your formations from song to song might be an effective "staging" change.
7. Be sure that the blend, balance, tuning, and overall musicality of a performance doesn't suffer because of your staging choices. If anything, your staging should strengthen all musical elements. Sometimes just having a choir move is the best way to ease vocal tension and sing a musical line.
8. Students must "own" every movement so that it looks natural. Staging and choreography only works if every singer looks comfortable with the chosen movement. Don't choreograph a staging movement that 10 people in your choir will never be able to achieve. Staging or movement

must match the talent level of the members in your group or choir.

9. Shy away from "cheesy" movements. Every move should have integrity and a purpose. You should be able to explain to your choir why you chose each movement and why it will enhance the text and overall performance.

10. Appropriate facial expression is not something that can be learned and implemented during the final week or two of rehearsals. Your singers should be showing facial expression for the text beginning at the first rehearsal. Facial expression on stage is muscle memory; and if it isn't something the singers have become comfortable with every day in rehearsal, it won't magically happen in performance.

In closing, I want to say how strongly I feel that learning all styles of music is imperatively important to building a well-rounded choral program. There are good and bad songs along with good and bad composers in all genres of music (including classical), and it is our job to find the gems in a variety of styles that will educate our students and entertain our audiences. Every genre of music can and should be performed with proper vocal technique and should also be educational for our students. It is our job as educators to expose our students to these different musical styles, to do the research on how to perform them properly, and to perform each piece of music with conviction and heartfelt emotion.

VOCAL COACHES

A great vocal coach is a rare breed, as this individual needs to walk into a room, form an immediate bond with a group of singers, and then address whatever needs addressing, which can draw upon composition, arranging, directing, psychology, etc. Consider coaches the Navy SEALs of vocal music: called upon for an important brief mission, given a short time to make a significant impact, then disappearing as quickly as they came. To leave a group changed, exhilarated, refocused, inspired after only a brief interaction is as much an art as a craft, requiring deep knowledge in addition to charisma.

Tom Carter

The problem of inconsistent emotion in choral music is not a new one. It inspired Tom Carter to tap into his experiences as a stage director and drama teacher while directing choral music, which resulted in the excellent book *Choral Charisma: Singing with Expression*. Tom is a frequent lecturer, coach, and clinician around North America, inspiring young singers and changing the nature of choral music performance one group at a time.

DEKE SHARON: How did you come to develop your theater-meets-choral technique?

TOM CARTER: As a frequent audience member at choir concerts in the '70s and '80s, I became more and more aware that I was not as engaged in the performances as I wanted to be. Looking at the concert through a stage director's lens, the reason was clear: the singers were not as engaged in their performances as they could have been.

In 1989, when Charlene Archibeque asked me to help the San Jose State University Choraliers with their stage presence (I'd been a member of the group the year before), I began using techniques that were similar to the ones I used with actors in my stage directing and teaching. I continued to work with the Choraliers and other groups for many years, fine-tuning the process.

DS: How do you approach singing with emotion?

TC: I invite singers to envision a story, real or imagined, that will give them a compelling reason to sing the song. To help them commit wholeheartedly, I look for opportunities for them to personalize and physicalize whenever possible.

For example, if the group is singing "This Little Light of Mine," the singers might think of someone specific who needs encouragement to break out of a particularly dark emotional place. When the group sings, they aren't thinking about expressing any particular emotion—they're trying to get their friend to "let [their light] shine."

For even more dynamic expression, I might suggest a group scenario like the following: The singers are collectively trying to get someone to join the choir—someone whose life would be totally transformed by joining. After creating the specifics of their story, the group can celebrate their own "shining" as they sing, smiling authentically at one another as they do so. "Get your neighbor to smile; share the love of singing with them" would give the singers an interpersonal objective to help them bring this song alive—and bring their new member into the fold.

To deepen the engagement, I've done things like having small groups of singers surround individual volunteers who are huddled on the floor in front of them. The singers sing the song while they try to encourage their friend to look up, cheer up, and ultimately *stand up*, joining the group.

Singers who use this type of process experience a wide range of emotions specifically tied to the text and music, emotions that arise from organic human behaviors. Their audiences are similarly engaged.

DS: What elements of Method acting translate directly into vocal music, and which do not translate?

TC: Since Method acting is the application of everyday behavior to performance, most elements translate immediately. After singers are reminded of the "Method acting" behaviors they actually use on a daily basis, they can directly incorporate them into their singing.

That said, I only use the core of the Method when I work with singers. Basically, this involves *creating a story* that supports the text, using *imagery* (seeing mental images related to our words), playing *objectives* (trying to affect other people), and—when helpful—the *use of the imagination* to act truthfully in imaginary circumstances. Since my goal is to support all singers regardless of age and experience, I only use Method acting techniques that are easily accessible.

DS: What are the challenges you find when approaching choirs for the first time with your method?

TC: While there's no challenge common to all groups, some singers have high levels of self-consciousness that prevent full commitment at the outset. I've found that creating an awareness of the inner critic begins to reduce the power it has over them, leading to less self-consciousness and more dynamic expression. Encouragement, open discussion, and risk-taking exercises can also be very helpful in helping them unleash their expressive potential.

While self-consciousness can limit a singer's initial commitment, an unsafe environment can stifle an entire choir's willingness to risk vulnerable expression. I've occasionally seen just a few singers create an environment so toxic that the entire group shuts down. When singers feel this threatened by their peers, it's often necessary to address the issue directly by identifying the problem, encouraging those who feel unsafe, and challenging those responsible to make more supportive choices.

When singers feel unsafe due to their *director's* anger, judgment, or perfectionism, it's the biggest challenge of all; unless the director changes, it's unlikely that the singers will risk anything but the most staid and reserved expression.

DS: What are the biggest traps a group can fall into when attempting to sing emotionally?

TC: Some traps include overacting, trying to impress the audience, and trying to manipulate the audience to feel a particular emotion—all of which will prevent the singers from expressing themselves in an honest or compelling fashion. While singers doing the above are "trying to affect other people," their *objectives* have crossed the footlights; since these particular traps result in singers trying to affect the audience directly, their behavior has become inauthentic and manipulative.

Ironically, "attempting to sing emotionally" can also be a trap in and of itself. When humans express emotions in real life, they're usually *not* "attempting to speak emotionally." Consequently, if singers literally "try to sing emotionally" for the audience, they end up doing something artificial—they end up *indicating* the emotion rather than experiencing it in its natural form. Then neither they nor the audience will be deeply moved. The key is to create an authentic emotional experience in the moment that has nothing to do with trying to affect the audience.

To avoid these traps, singers and directors might choose to be very cautious whenever they address "singing with emotion." Likewise, singers can be very aware of their specific thought processes when they sing. This way they can pull themselves out if they notice that they're falling into one of the traps.

Christopher Diaz

Christopher Diaz is the kind of a cappella Renaissance man that makes for the ideal coach: he led his college group, All-Night Yahtzee, to three consecutive ICCA finals, where he won awards as a soloist and arranger; won many CARAs; trained as a classical vocalist; produced a cappella events and podcasts; frequently judges both recorded and live a cappella; worked behind the scenes on *The Sing-Off*; and most recently joined forces with other a cappella all-stars to form the Exchange, who are now one of contemporary a cappella's most successful groups internationally. He sees a cappella from all sides.

DEKE SHARON: You sang collegiate a cappella at Florida State University while getting a degree in vocal performance. How did each of those experiences inform your own emotional performing? Were they ever at odds?

CHRISTOPHER DIAZ: On the one hand, the world of classical singing is pretty clear in its devotion to a specific vocal technique and production style, which I learned over the course of my time at the school, absorbing the many skills and techniques. On the other hand, such devotion to a technique and a curriculum overflowing with language, song literature, workshops, lessons, and opera and recital rehearsals doesn't often leave time to sit and ponder the "why" of the music. The faculty wasn't always thrilled that, with such a full schedule, I would spend so much of my precious remaining time on non-classical music endeavors.

Luckily, a requirement for my degree was that I sing in a choir. It was there, in the University Singers under the direction of Dr. Kevin Fenton, that I really cultivated an appreciation for the emotional resonance of vocal music. It was rehearsing, and then eventually performing, with him that inspired my expectation for what could be reveled in, or wrestled or coaxed out of a piece of music. He is the kind of director that spends a fair and focused amount of time on teaching the music, setting articulations and expressions and otherwise preparing the choir, but it is in his coaching and conducting of those pieces that his genuine and passionate engagement with the material really shines. I remember him conjuring the image of a Russian peasant woman trudging through the snow for food, humming to herself for comfort the same Rachmaninoff hymn that we were singing together. This illumination of the connection we all stand to make through music was profound and carried over into my work with All-Night Yahtzee.

My time with All-Night Yahtzee was emotionally profound in a different but related way. If my time in choir was where I really came to understand the philosophy behind group singing, Yahtzee was where I learned to implement it, and where I felt its effects. I remember the first time I ever sang isolated chords with this group—perhaps ever, now that I think about it—and being genuinely shocked by how bonded the other singers and I were. Our musicality moved as simultaneously as our emotional responses to the music. That sense of connection was and is thrilling to me.

DS: You're known for the emotional aspect of your coaching. Why do you think this is, and why do you focus on emotion?
CD: Many directors focus almost exclusively on the technical aspects of their music-making, and while every singing group wants to be pitch perfect (I won't apologize for the pun, not here!) a technically perfect performance from a group is often lacking the one thing that makes it any good: its humanity. I believe that an understanding of what and why you are singing should be firmly at the heart of all of the technical and musical decisions you will make.

To speak generally, a singer performing in an a cappella group has some baseline of musical knowledge. Whether or not she grasps these concepts by name, she understands pitch, rhythm, dynamics, and tuning. To learn, memorize, polish, and perform a song a cappella is a time-consuming and energy-intensive feat. As a coach who often doesn't have much more than an hour at a time with a group, I have to first trust in the inherent skills of the singers and second be able to clearly communicate to them how to use those skills more efficiently toward their performance goals.

The average audience member is not so concerned with the musical perfection of a performance. Consistently across the spectrum of live musical performance it is the performance that combines both technical prowess and emotional resonance that stands out. It is why Adele and Sam Smith's subtly piquant performances stand easily among the greatest of our current generation. With that in mind, I try to help singers see the patterns in those performances that they may not have noticed before, and usually that pattern is one consistent with emotional engagement from the performers. Again, every singer wants to be as good as he or she can be, but it shouldn't be at the expense of the story you're telling.

DS: For a long time you had a popular podcast that would review a cappella albums (*Mouth Off!*). How do you find recorded vocal music differs from live, and what challenges does each face when presenting emotionally powerful performances?
CD: Obviously, live music has layers of visual and sensory stimulation that aren't present when you listen to a recording. There is no substitute for the way the smell of a café informs the sound of a voice you're hearing singing there, or the way the construction materials of a hall (or lack of a hall) will change the resonance of the tones. In this way, some might say that recorded music is inferior to live music in its singularity, and I would mostly agree. But we can't all afford to go to concerts every night.

Like it or not, music has had to adapt to the portable, digital revolution so that we can have more of it more of the time. With that adaptation has come compression, file degradation, and other negative technical impositions on the raw beauty and power of music. But it has also made readily available the entire world's music, and has therefore opened the world up to a whole new library of stories.

As both a reviewer on *Mouth Off!* and a coach, I have come across dozens and dozens of perfectly sung, well arranged, beautifully produced songs and albums of all styles that are profoundly forgettable. That is simply because they lack the emotional sincerity of a real story or storyteller, and do not reach out with that invisible feelings-hand to greet the distant audience. The great challenge of recorded music is finding a way to infuse the soul, spontaneity, and sincerity not just of a live performance, but of the human performing it, into a track.

Obviously, innumerable artists have cracked the code, without which we wouldn't have a music industry to speak of. In the vocal music realm, the same stands, but in this new wave of contemporary a cappella, the speed with which one can learn recording and production basics doesn't always jibe with the real-time growth of one's own maturity, skills, or self-awareness. So we, faultless, make mostly cover songs that are pretty because they are pretty. And that's okay. But they are ultimately forgettable until we infuse them with the essence of "us," and our voices alone won't do it. We have to draw out the intangible humanity of the songs we sing, and to do that we only have to turn to the words and music.

DS: You now tour the world performing with the Exchange, sharing the stage with the Backstreet Boys, performing for people of different nationalities, sometimes without an understanding of English. Do you find different countries react differently emotionally to your performances? Do you find their understanding and enjoyment changes if they can't understand the lyrics?

CD: I could just say that in my experience Taiwanese audience members are very reserved until you give them permission to go nuts—and then they do. I could say simply that Germans are good clappers (two and four almost always, my friends), and that Australians are quiet but open-minded audiences. I could say confidently that Spaniards have some of the loudest cheers, and could state flatly that New Yorkers usually seem pretty bored until you're setting yourself on fire. But to just make a set of general statements undermines the truth I've learned throughout my travels about the reality of what we do as storytellers.

Getting to perform on stage for diverse crowds, especially those abroad, has helped me (and many times forced me) to understand that storytelling is the backbone of most of what we do as artists. While music can fairly be considered a universal language, at the heart of it in this context is usually a human. That human, despite everything that appears to the contrary, is quite a bit like you and me. She has her own unique experiences in life, certainly, but in times of crisis feels all of the same emotions as you or me. All humans, regardless of our language or appearance, pull from a vast pool of shared emotional responses and experiences. This is evidenced by the universality of human facial expressions across races and ethnicities. Joy, sorrow, anger, and my personal favorite, surprise, are all universal around the globe when authentically felt. Throughout history, all of our stories in all of our many different languages have talked about, primarily, the same sorts of feelings and situations: love, life, death, joy, wonder, fear, doubt. We are connected by these feelings.

So, rather than tasking the audience with the cerebral processes of translation and interpretation before enjoyment, the Exchange and I try to bypass the brain and go straight for the heart. By recognizing and taking advantage of our universal human responses to stimulus, e.g., fight or flight, we can act deliberately to tell our stories with an engaged, empathetic outlook. Sure, there are times when a pop song, often already lacking in any meaningful dramatic or emotional content, or a quick English-language pun or anachronism will go "over the head" of a foreign-language-speaking crowd. Generally speaking, though, most audiences can identify with any performance that has a determined sense of emotional identity, a charismatic and authentic delivery, and a good beat.

DS: You've coached groups on four continents. Do you find there to be differences in the approach to music in different cultures? Are there universalities?

CD: There are piles of each! The reality is that any group of people, regardless of nationality or culture, will have unique characteristics that will in turn inform unique performance choices. That said, a group's approach to music-making, and to art in general, has much to do with the way each of the singers' parents raised them to perceive music, and with his or her culture's attitude toward music. A culture's attitude toward music is usually substantially influenced by its shared social, religious, political, geographical, and artistic history. Generally, in places where the shared history has put an emphasis on music as 1) a social bonding tool and 2) an educational tool, the average quality of musicianship tends to be higher. There is also the matter of biological/racial/ethnic homogeneity and its effects on vocal production, education, government, policy, and the social treatment and perception of music (among other things).

I have observed that in the East Asian countries of Hong Kong, Taiwan, Singapore and Japan, many young people view music as more of an educational tool than a diversion. The same could be said of many countries in Europe, and around the world. But, taken on their own, these observations miss a bigger point: that a culture's attitude toward music is, in my opinion, the biggest influence on a group's approach to music-making. In many Asian and European cultures, children grow up playing piano or violin, learning music theory, and using song as a learning device in various subjects. Aside from this, in many of these cultures music is also used as a social bonding tool. Folk stories and many religious and family mythologies and histories are passed down through song. Weddings and funerals, births and birthdays, holidays and leisurely hangouts are punctuated, enhanced, and oftentimes driven by communal musical expression. If you combine what might be perceived as a sort of ennui or "boredom" with institutional music at the primary level with what some might perceive as a kind of social shyness or reservation, one might perceive a quiet or insecure group. I have found in those situations that I have had to simply use a specific and deliberate combination of energy, engagement, and exercises to get a response from a given group from this demographic.

In America or Australia, though, where music programs vary widely from state to state, there isn't really a standard I've noticed in terms of "music-making." There is definitely a higher sense of "enjoyment" of the music, meaning but not limited to a more extroverted performance manner. There is also a greater perception of music as a pleasure or hobby, not as a tool. And I find, generally speaking, that scholastic groups in America are behind their Asian and European counterparts when it comes to a baseline of technical ability and knowledge of theory, though they quite often excel at accessing that intangible yet essential mystique ever present in good storytelling.

Based on these observations, it would be prudent to note that music and arts education is grossly underfunded in the United States, and this fact could perhaps account for an achievement gap. That said, music is one of this country's most lucrative exports, boasting as of 2013 a $15.1 billion dollar industry. Perhaps there is some connection between the relative emotional and social extroversion of Americans and the emotional resonance of their music.

DS: What advice do you have for other coaches hoping to inspire great emotional performances from the groups they're working with?

CD: Be compassionate. Singing is actually really hard. It calls for the simultaneous management of almost all of one's senses, along with a host of involved cerebral processes to keep it sounding like something people want to hear. Understand that it might take explaining and/or trying something a couple of different ways with a group or singer before they get it. Sometimes they don't get it. It's okay. This is a cappella. It's supposed to be fun! And the same story can be told and received in innumerable ways.

Model things. It's one thing to talk about the sound you want, and it's another thing to demonstrate the sound you want. To be a good model for your groups, you have to sing a lot yourself and develop the same kind of control over your own instrument that you expect from your singers.

Sing. A lot. This probably seems like a given, but many coaches and directors don't do it enough. Just singing in your car, in the shower, or doing dishes will help you build both your skills and endurance. It'll also help you build a richer history of personal vocal experiences to pull from when working with a group. You'll have more ways to explain how to do something, or how not to do something.

Be assertive, but not aggressive. As a coach, time management is critical. You can't allow for a senatorial vote in the alto section about the shape of a vowel, or nitpick with a music director about the role of diphthongs in a song, or whatever. Your job is to efficiently offer a snapshot or reflection of the group and give them some critical feedback and actionable suggestions that will elevate their performance. That is a tall order for only an hour. Singers are empathetic, passion-driven creatures—we like to see and feel your passion for your principles and methods, but we don't want to feel assaulted by your aggressive implementation.

Make mistakes. This is the most important thing that I have done and continue to do as a coach. I make mistakes during my coachings right along with the singers. This connects us on a social level where the singing may not—and opens the doors for trust. I make mistakes not on purpose, usually, but because I will attempt to sing along or model something with full conviction. Sometimes it doesn't work, but again, this is unavoidable. Singing is hard. No matter how many wonder stories we read about child prodigies and singers with a golden throat since birth—they are the exceptions and not the rules. The rest of us have to work really hard and make a lot of mistakes in our development so that we can build our craft.

Hannah Juliano

I first met Hannah when she was a teenager, as I was directing her mother, Raeleen, in Groove 66 (later Vybration) at Disneyland, and it was clear from the start that there was something special about this kid. Voracious for knowledge, she wanted to know the best music schools in the country as a sixteen-year-old. It was not long before she was performing on *The Sing-Off*, first as a member of Berklee Pitch Slapped, then later as a member of Delilah. She directed both groups beautifully, which is why I invited her to join the staff at Camp A Cappella, then to become my assistant for Vocalosity. Hannah is one of the rare people who has it all, on and off stage, and understands how to bring the best out of singers.

DEKE SHARON: With a professional singer/performer for a mother and so much music in your life, how did your musical experiences in school compare to music outside of school? What did you learn from each?

HANNAH JULIANO: In high school, I learned how to work on a team. I learned how to follow a director, how to be someone my fellow band members or choir members could lean on, and how to eventually direct them myself. I learned how to balance my schedule between playing a sport and being in the musical.

In college, I learned that I had previously been a big fish in a small pond. It was a huge, amazing, humbling reality check and made me want to work hard at expanding my knowledge and experience. Being a member of the a cappella group there felt like "outside of school," and sometimes it was. We ran the music, the rehearsals, the business, the finances all ourselves. I learned how hard it was to try to direct my friends, how to separate business and friendship. I didn't do a very good job at it sometimes, which led to big life lessons in management, responsibility, humility, and what it takes to lead.

Outside of school was a big, flashy blur. I learned about the world of reality television. I learned how to look at the big picture, how to stop sweating the small details, how being true to yourself instead of trying to be what you think someone else wants is always going to feel better (and work better).

DS: What are the best things you learned at Berklee College of Music? What did you learn that you needed to unlearn?

HJ: Most of the pivotal lessons were from Pitch Slapped, singing and arranging and directing that group. I had to learn deadlines, group politics, how to choreograph, how to keep everyone happy, how to be their leader and their friend, which was more important at specific times. Responsibility on top of creativity. I put a lot of pressure on myself to make everyone happy instead of just doing the job of leading them when needed. That was a tough lesson to learn.

Things that I unlearned? I've found that working in music is very different in the ways you communicate with other musicians. We all come from different places, learn differently, understand music differently, communicate differently . . . it's like we speak different languages. Having a career in music means learning how to say the same things in different languages. Working in the world involves first figuring out which languages the people you're working with speak, and then creating music together that speaks in many different languages for people to receive and enjoy.

Music education also feels a lot like learning music backwards. You learn how to define and create shortcuts for the things that we hear naturally as humans. We instinctively know what a turnaround is, but when we study we focus in on it, learn the characteristics of it, and study it until we understand it and it becomes natural in our playing and writing.

DS: As a young working musician, do you feel you had to sacrifice any musicality or emotional sincerity to fit into the current marketplace?

HJ: I don't believe so. There's never a lack of sincerity; it's all a matter of finding the right blend of skills, work, and heart. As a working professional musician, in a large, bustling, expensive city, I'm not going to get 100 percent music satisfaction, 100 percent coworker buddies, and 100 percent cash in the bank on every gig. It's not always a matter of talent or taste. So I take pleasure in every job I do, from singing at weddings, to orchestrating for Broadway stars, to hearing a Pepsi ad echo my voice back to me during the Super Bowl.

What you sacrifice is your own self-consciousness. But not sincerity—the sincerity is in the honest work that you do. If you come at any job you do, no matter how cool or ridiculous you think it is, with an earnest attempt to make it better for others and deliver a product you would be proud of in whatever way, then there's nothing to sacrifice.

DS: Having worked with many professional singers and groups, what have you learned from their practices and processes that makes you a more effective emotional musician? What do they do that you have learned isn't effective?

HJ: The really good ones have spent so much time learning and failing and working and honing and rehearsing, they are heroes. They are dependable, whether you like them as a person or not. They will be there early, with a banana and two bottles of water. They rarely need sheet music unless it's last-minute. They are prepared, not just with the music, but prepared to roll with any changes. I learned that if it feels like too much work for the money, then you either need to sacrifice the job or accept that you'll work hard for a product no matter what, and you won't always be able to be compensated properly. Something's gotta give.

Emotionally, I've noticed that most professionals remain emotionless when being critiqued, yet still put lots of emotion in their performance. It's hard to hear the word "no" audition after audition, but everyone who works in this business goes through it. You gotta learn how to get around it, how to separate the opinion from the situation from the work from the heart. Once you do, it makes life and work a lot easier to navigate emotionally.

DS: You have worked as a session singer, arranger, composer, music director, vocal coach, and all-around mentor. What advice do you have for people in any of these pursuits when it comes to creating emotionally powerful music?

HJ: Do everything with intent! Try to have a reason for everything. Every choice, every intuition in your process should be looked at, decided on, and accepted with mindful intent.

Performing with empathy is your friend. If you are in a situation singing about an experience that you have never been through, pull apart the emotions that are represented that are more than "happy" or "sad" or "angry." That can be very powerful for you and for an audience, because you are using your personal experience to express the experience of another, which in turn helps others experience and express. Sing for a friend who has gone through something similar to help you better understand it all. Honestly emoting in music is one of the most powerful tools we have.

If you want to be a professional, you will eventually have to balance it all. Balance that which you love, that which you are great at, that which you are paid for, and that which the audience (or boss) needs. Balance is the key, as always.

In the end, the professionals come at everything from an intentional, emotional standpoint. We all love music. We all want to be great at it. We all want to be recognized for it. We all want to expand the music we love and share it with as many people as we can. When your foundation is that passion and that curiosity for more, then everything you do will be infused with emotion, with a little piece of you swirled in.

DS: In Vocalosity, you're the assistant music director as well as a performer. How do you remain focused on your own emotional performance while analyzing others at the same time?
HJ: I wear both hats; it just depends on which hat is on top at which time. Throughout a rehearsal, recording session, or video shoot, I have to switch back and forth, which can be exhausting if it's all personally emotionally charged. I try to be as prepared as possible, know the music, and take care of my personal responsibilities ahead of time so they don't overlap. Then it's easier to turn on the fun when I am performing because I'm not stressing about getting the music right. The director is always making sure everything sounds right and is on track, but the performer is having fun and delivering the music.

Most of it comes with practice. Every group I've been in, I've always thought about the big picture first, and my own individual part in it much further back. A big part is the preparation that goes in beforehand so I don't self-critique my every move. It allows me to shift my gaze a little further up; I know what it's all supposed to sound like, and who's doing what, so I just follow along while singing my part and take mental note on where things pop up and are a little off or out of place. And if something comes up that's unexpected and wonderful, keep it!

GROUPS

A great vocal harmony group is pure magic. Soaring melodies, rich harmonies, ringing overtones, multiple lead singers: an embarrassment of riches. Obviously, this kind of breathtaking excellence does not just happen, although each of today's biggest vocal groups took very different paths, and met different challenges, on the road to success.

Home Free

Sometimes it takes a while for a new combination to catch on, but in the case of Home Free, the marriage of country and a cappella has resulted in almost immediate success, including duets with legends like the Oak Ridge Boys and Kenny Rogers, viral videos, chart-topping albums, and appearances at the Grand Ole Opry. Before all the fame, they were a journeyman a cappella group: school assemblies, cruise ships, corporate gigs, singing pop and rock, hoping for their big break.

DEKE SHARON: Country music is in many ways modern American folk music, with clear themes: big party, big joy, big loss, big sadness. Do you find it easier to perform than pop or rock?

TIM FOUST: Yep. It's mostly just storytelling. And the choruses tend to arrange themselves—standard three-part, everyone-sings-the-lyrics harmony.

ADAM RUPP: On the emotional side, that question goes back to who you are and how you connect to the genre with its ideas and themes.

AUSTIN BROWN: Growing up on a dirt road, and always singing along with a natural twang, yeah, I find it way easier to sing country music.

CHRIS RUPP: One of the things that we discovered when we really started delving into country music is how good music is good music, and vice versa, no matter the genre. What I mean by that is that there are deep, meaningful songs in pop or country or blues or art song or whatever genre you're looking at; you just need to find those songs.

DS: You are five different individuals. How do you come together to approach a song emotionally in the same way?

CR: I don't think we look at it as five different individuals; we're one whole unit being directed by whoever is leading the way with the solo. While internally we may have our own stories to use as motivation, as a whole unit we respond to whoever is singing lead, feeding off the direction they are taking it, feeling their ebb and flow, and responding accordingly.

AR: Whoever is arranging or taking lead on a song starts the proposition. Then whoever gets the passion will go from there.

AB: Once a song gets in our bones, when the muscle memory takes over, only then do I start to truly feel what the fiber of a song is and where it can go.

TF: We make sure that each arrangement has at least one moment that moves all of us.

DS: How much control over the mood of a song does the arranger have? The soloist?

AB: For me an arrangement is a starting point. A guideline. It can never (in Home Free at least) be a rigid law that can't be broken. As we've grown the past couple of years, my favorite arrangements of ours are the ones that are built after the soloist has solidified the basic feel and best key for himself.

CR: The arranger can certainly set the mood or style of a song, which then creates a platform for the soloist to take it in his own direction. But it also can be reversed and sent back to the drawing board if the band isn't feeling it.

AR: We typically let those with the passion take lead on the emotional direction of the song, but remember an arranger can only instruct intentions and it's up to the performers or soloist to execute.

DS: How do your relationships behind the scenes affect your performances?

AB: Our relationships do affect our performances on stage greatly, for the most part in a good way. As we grow more and more together, spending much more time with each other than any of

our family or friends, that bond and deep understanding of one another translates to comfort and a very liberating freedom onstage.
AR: We spent eight hours in New York during one of our tours to do
some resolutions and goal setting, and the result was astonishing as
to how much better we performed and functioned together. Everyone chose three out of 100 cards with varying one-word ideas,
themes, or qualities that tell us what matters most in our lives, a
way to understand someone and what they value most. Then, one
at a time, everyone expressed whatever really, I mean really, was
bothering them about someone else. Having a third party that is
someone everyone looked up to really helped. But, after each issue
was really dug into, with everyone expressing themselves honestly,
we collectively found a set of acceptable like-minded resolutions
and goals for the group. The result was the best we have ever been
in tune and the best energy we have ever brought on stage. Plus, it
affected all other aspects of our work, because we understand each
other more and what is most important in our lives. Coming from
that perspective about someone instead of creating stories of your
own and your own false impressions makes for progress.

DS: Much of your success has come on screen (*The Sing-Off*, You-
Tube). How do you find the process of emoting and performing for
camera different from a live audience?
CR: When you're on stage you are always getting live and direct
feedback from the audience. However, once you're behind a camera, that feedback is either nonexistent or minimal, so you have
less to gauge with.
TF: Cameras capture subtleties that would otherwise go unnoticed.
In a live show, we have to emote to the people in the last row.
AB: What you feel doesn't necessarily translate to what your face
looks like you are feeling. The most important on-camera lesson
I ever learned was to watch yourself more . . . which we haven't
been doing for lack of time and, to a degree, lack of experience. If
you believe yourself on camera, then it's probably believable; we
are our harshest critics.

DS: On your many frequent national tours, do you find it difficult
to generate emotion song after song, night after night? How do
you remain focused?
TF: Unfortunately, there are some nights that I just don't feel like
performing. When this happens, I'll look around the audience and

find the face of someone who is having one of the best nights of their life. It cures me instantly. It's particularly effective when it is a small child. I think about what an important moment this would have been for me at that age. Suddenly I'm compelled to give the best performance of my life.

CR: Also, no song is ever 100 percent perfect . . . there are always areas to improve on, and working on nailing that one riff a bit better or doing that staging a bit crisper can help you maintain your focus as well.

AB: If you are doing your job right, the audience will give every bit of energy you could ever need to remain focused. They will listen if you tell them to scream. They will applaud louder if you pull it out of them. So, if they start to fade, it's your job to get out of your comfort zone and find a way to bring their excitement back.

DS: What's your advice to a group that wants to create emotionally compelling performances?

TF: You have to know the music inside and out. If you're thinking about the notes, even in the slightest, you're not performing. Then you have to allow the music to compel you emotionally. Stop focusing on how it sounds, and embrace how it feels. Then share that feeling with your audience. It's infectious.

CR: Learning the notes on the page is only half the challenge. You also need to make sure you're telling a story, whatever that may be. Is that story being conveyed to the audience? If you are able to tell that story, *that's* when you will truly connect with your audience and will have a much greater impact than a technically correct but emotionally lacking performance.

AR: When we put our show together, we look at the flow, making sure it keeps the music going and doesn't get stale with talking. Talking over a vamp, stopping the song for a step out, putting in breakdowns, teasing the start of a song. Watch other great concerts live to see what the artist does that isn't in the recording that will make everyone there think, "Wow. That was special and I was there to see it. I can't wait to tell everyone about what they did." Be creative, take chances, trial and error. Being an artist is all about expression and breaking boxes, and people who come to a show aren't there to watch you "play the recording."

AB: Make music you want to make, and make it for yourself. Don't make music you think other people want you to make. Don't make music you think "most" people will like. Don't make a certain kind of music or choose to cover a certain song just because it's what's popular right now. Sure, that can be a great business plan in the right context. But absolutely, totally, with all the serious direction I can give, do not begin crafting your art from a place seeking success or notoriety. Begin your art from a place that gives you joy, fulfillment, and most importantly, fun. When you find an audience that loves the music you are making for yourself, go with them. And give them more and more. The audience will be ever so much more loyal over the years, and in time so too will your joy and the genuine emotional expression that can be experienced as a performer and musician.

Manhattan Transfer

There isn't a vocal harmony group working today that doesn't owe a debt to the pioneering work of the Manhattan Transfer, who opened countless doors and showed the U.S. market that vocal harmony could span styles and still be a huge commercial success. With 29 albums and a career spanning six decades, the group continues to tour and inspire generations of singers around the world.

DEKE SHARON: You made your initial splash during the 1970s, when a cappella and other vocal harmony singing was at a nadir, and continue to defy genre classification, singing pop, doo-wop, bebop, disco, funk, swing, Brazilian, close harmony, Christmas music, a cappella . . . probably the most diverse cross-section of styles for a Grammy-winning and *Billboard* charting act in the history of popular music. To what do you attribute this success and flexibility?

MANHATTAN TRANSFER: Our initial success in the '70s was a combination of how we sounded, how we looked, our presentation, our staunch determination, and the help of a lot of people who believed in us. Musically, MT was always very eclectic. All of us were exposed to various genres of music, and we didn't feel we had to limit ourselves to just one style, nor did we want to get labeled into a particular musical bag. We were very fortunate to get signed to Atlantic Records by its founder and CEO, Ahmet Ertegun. Ahmet understood the group's musical sensibilities and allowed us to explore as artists. This gave us the flexibility and freedom to apply our vocal harmony to various styles of music.

DS: When performing in different styles, do you find the emotional elements of your performance shifting, or do the same principles apply regardless? How much of the emotion in your music is discussed and planned, and how much is unspoken, the result of having sung together for 40 years?

MT: Every song requires a point of view, an origin and interpretation that is true to us. It can be determined by a lyric, a groove, or a style of music. We approach our singing like an actor does a role. We set certain parameters of interpretation to be true to the form. For example, crooning a ballad, stylistically, is very different from singing R&B, swing, doo-wop, or vocalese jazz or improvisation. We don't talk about the emotions in our music, because they are conveyed instinctively. We naturally blend because we know how to match our voices with one another, and usually the vocal arrangement will indicate the ebb and flow of the dynamics.

DS: You have done many fantastic covers over the years, putting your own spin on jazz and pop classics. How you do as a group determine the musical and emotional direction of your versions?
MT: It all depends on the song and what our goal for the song is. With jazz, especially with vocalese, we followed the wisdom that Jon Hendricks conveyed to us:

"The most important thing to do in singing vocalese is to go back to the source and vocally interpret what the original instrumentalists played. The words are secondary, because in many cases the lyrics go by so fast that the listener is not going to understand them."

On the other side of the spectrum with pop music, the focus usually was on making a record that would get played on the radio. A lot had to do with the vocal and instrumental arrangement, hand-picking the right musicians and the production. For example, with "Boy from New York City," Alan wrote the vocal arrangement and wanted to capture the essence of the original recording by the Adlibs, but also wanted to change it up to make it unique for us. Jay Graydon added a guitar lick that gave it a contemporary edge, but emotionally the track was missing a drive that our demo had. We decided to do another track with a different drummer, and that made all the difference. "Boy from New York City" went on to number three on the *Billboard* pop charts and won us a Grammy.

DS: The founder of your group, Tim Hauser, passed away in October 2014. How did that affect the group emotionally?
MT: Tim, Janis, and Alan were singing partners for 44 years, Cheryl for 35 years, and we felt a tremendous gap and loss. There were times when we lost it on stage and couldn't sing. We contemplated ending the group but decided that we wanted to continue the legacy of music we worked so hard to create, and this is what we believe Tim would want as well. We have been very fortunate to have Trist Curless join us. Trist has an extensive vocal group background; he is the cofounder of the cappella group m-pact and is a wonderful addition to MT.

DS: You've performed around the world for decades. Have you seen a change in the emotional reaction to your music based on geography or demographics or different generations?

MT: With the passage of time, we see how our fans feel great nostalgia with us and our music. Because of the instability in the world today, we seem to represent a sense of normalcy and calm amidst the chaos and insanity the world is confronted with. We are viewed as ambassadors of good will. Also, because of the renewed interest in vocal harmony in high schools and universities especially here in the U.S., the demographics of our audience are expanding and getting younger. We were pioneers that paved the way and these young singers want to come and hear us live.

Pentatonix

If there is one a cappella group that needs no introduction in the year of this book's publication, it's Pentatonix. From their humble beginnings meeting each other for the first time the night before *Sing-Off* auditions to their domination of modern media (10 million subscribers on YouTube and counting), PTX are the standard bearers of the contemporary a cappella style. Before they were superstars, they were just five kids in high school choir who loved to sing.

DEKE SHARON: You all sang in choir in school. Do you recall any particularly emotional school performances, and if so what made them emotionally powerful?

MITCH GRASSI: I remember one particular instance when I felt very moved by the music. I was selected to be a member of the Texas All-State Choir, and that year we were performing a version of "Sanctus" that was especially memorable because of its arced song structure. It started very subdued and beautiful, and then it began to build and build until it reached an incredibly powerful, emotional crux. Then it slowly, steadily faded away. I remember the night of the actual performance when we performed the piece, and when we reached the peak, everyone in the room could feel it. It was electric, cathartic.

AVI KAPLAN: When I was at Mt. San Antonio College, our choir was invited to the National ACDA convention. We worked all year to get our set to where it was the night of the performance. The goal for the entire choir was to change people's lives with music. We gave everything we had that night, and after we finished the entire audience was in tears and so were we. I'll never forget that performance as long as I live.

SCOTT HOYING: In our chamber choir, we sang an Eric Whitacre piece called "A Boy and a Girl." The harmonies were so lush, and our choir had so many amazing singers, I remember being brought to tears one day when we were rehearsing it.

KEVIN OLUSOLA: I remember a song I sang in my fifth grade choir called "Circle Round the Moon," by Mark Hierholzer. It moved me so much because of the joyous nature of the tune. All I could ever do was smile every single time the chorus of the song came around.

DS: Your online presence is legendary, and although your technique is superlative, the way you make people feel is what keeps them coming back time and again to hear your music. How do you reach through the camera and touch people's hearts?

SH: We just have fun! We arrange what we think is great, we come up with video concepts we think are great, and we perform as best we can. Most importantly, we enjoy doing it. I think people are drawn to the fact we are doing what we love and it's not contrived or forced.

KO: I think we've realized that what makes a cappella so special is the combination of the visual and the audio. You have to see the beatboxer creating beats with his mouth, you have to watch the bass singer hit those low notes, you have to pay attention to the tight harmonies. Therefore, we decided to utilize resources like YouTube to give people the audio and visual aspects of our performances. Our video concepts may differ from time to time, but it always comes back to the common theme of five people singing into a camera. I think just by singing to people very candidly like that, it makes people feel like they have a connection with us that's special. We love it.

MG: We like to remind our audience that we are, at the end of the day, simply music lovers. Just like them. We share common ground, and that sense of humanity is a big reason why we're often able to connect emotionally with our viewers. We don't like to appear intangible. We also just love connecting with the fans, in general, whether it be in person, on social media, etc.

AK: I think people really connect with us because we truly are ourselves and we genuinely connect with the music as a group.

DS: When rehearsing, you obviously learn all the notes. How do you prepare emotionally, and how does it affect your arranging and performing?

SH: All of us have complex lives with our own worries, doubts, joys, fears, etc., and depending on the piece, we apply those emotions to our performance. We have emotional, tearful heart-to-hearts about what each song means to us.

KO: We discuss what the song means to us so that we're all in the same emotional head space. That's what we did on *The Sing-Off* for "Dog Days Are Over." We all felt so connected to each other, and it made the performance that much more powerful.

AK: The emotional aspect of an arrangement and performance is extremely important. We as a group always try to capture the essence of a song and accentuate it. In order to do that, you have to first truly know what it's about. We base everything off of it.

MG: The emotional intent of each song really does drive the arrangement and vocal performance. Music and lyrics, in our case, are to be equally complementary to one another. We'll sit down, analyze the lyrics, and brainstorm ways we can really bring them to life and make them impactful through the arrangement.

DS: Recording and performing live are very different processes. How do you approach keeping the emotion central to each?

KO: For us, it's just staying connected to the story line that brings out the emotion in us. If we can do that, we will be able to express ourselves in each process.

AK: Keeping the emotional central in recording is the same as live. You keep it in the forefront of your mind.

SH: When I record, a lot of the time I close my eyes and picture being on stage. I can always feel a shift in the way I'm singing. I think it gets me out of my head and lets me just perform effortlessly and more emotionally.

MG: For me, it's easier to emote when I'm on stage in front of a crowd rather than in a recording studio. It's very crucial, though, to make sure your emotional intent comes across in recordings, because that's what the fans hear first, and that's what they'll listen to over and over. We're very detail-oriented, especially when it comes to inflection and emotional nuance in our songs.

DS: How do you shift between very different styles and moods as you go from song to song on stage?

KO: Lots and lots of practice. It's just practicing getting into the mind-set of the next piece.

SH: I think, having rehearsed all the songs so much, it just becomes muscle memory. I will say, though, that as I have toured I've noticed little nuances in the way I sing (when to belt, when to go into falsetto, when to bring my volume way down, etc.) that excite an audience, and I usually hold on to those as we tour.

AK: You have to be able to connect to each song extremely quickly. We do this by having a personal experience or image in our mind that reflects the vibe of the song to help us connect on a deep personal level.

MG: I think it's fairly intuitive. A certain groove (or lack of groove) puts me in a particular mind-set, and I perform appropriately to that style. It's all about connecting to and enjoying what you're performing! If you're enjoying it, the crowd will, too.

SH: In general, I think performing music is so incredible because it teaches you to embrace and *enjoy* an emotion and experience it vividly. Whether it be sadness, heartbreak, happiness, anger . . . you're accepting that emotion and honoring it. I think that can be applied to everyday life and teach us not to fight away sadness or anger, but to embrace it, accept it, and see it more as a guide.

Straight No Chaser

If you read it in a novel you wouldn't believe it: 10 years after performing, a member of a collegiate a cappella group posts a performance of "The Twelve Days of Christmas" online, and before long they've got a record deal, quit their various jobs, put the group back together, and become one of the most successful touring acts, selling more tickets than many rock bands. Now they have many *Billboard* charting albums and duets with some of the biggest names in music, and continue to pave the way for young aspiring a cappella groups. When looking at all the various aspects of the recent rise in a cappella, in many categories Straight No Chaser was first.

DEKE SHARON: Yours was the very first viral a cappella video. What do you think it was about your performance that grabbed people, and what is it in general about a cappella videos that people find so compelling?

SEGGIE ISHO: I think the rawness of the video is what got people so attached. At a time when everything was so polished and perfect, the "Twelve Days" video had a feeling of genuine realness to it.

DON NOTTINGHAM: One of the critical elements of our success has been that we are very relatable. That first video wasn't polished, it wasn't professional . . . it wasn't even particularly well recorded. But what people saw was 10 guys that looked like people they'd want to be friends with. We weren't pretentious, and we weren't putting on airs—we were just fun.

JEROME COLLINS: The video gave insight into exactly the type of guys we were: a raw talented bunch who just enjoyed performing together. Our grassroots, homegrown story is what made us more likeable to our audience and viewers. Everyone is in on the joke, and it's clean humor.

WALTER CHASE: I think it had something to do with the history behind that performance. You see an organized group singing something clever and having a good time doing it. "Where did these guys come from?"

STEVE MORGAN: As for a cappella videos' appeal (in general), I think people are still amazed at what the human voice can do. Sure, there are more and more examples available online these days, but groups continue to push the envelope with their creativity. Vocal percussion, alone, has become so intricate and entrenched in modern arrangements that people can hear almost any genre of music done a cappella and find drums and other percussion approximated so perfectly that they don't really miss anything from the original instrumental version of the song.

DS: Your fans are not typical teenage fan girls yet are legendarily devoted. How as performers do you connect with and foster that relationship, both on and off stage?

WC: Our fans, who lovingly call themselves "Chasers," are the greatest fans in music. They come to shows. They share videos they took at shows. They defend us online. They demand more content. They make us want to work harder. What we give in return is simple: We give the Chasers what they want. We do signing lines after every show—something we have done since college and something we do even if it's an arena show. We show the group behind the scenes—podcasts, Periscope sound checks, video the tour buses. We break the fourth wall and let the audience in on the joke—and we don't take ourselves too seriously.

SI: On stage, there is no fourth wall; we make that very clear from the opening video. As soon as we set foot on stage, we don't set foot on stage as performer and you as audience member; rather, we get out there and we're all friends. We are all in this show together. In addition, we fully encourage people to take pictures and video throughout the show. We're not singing to tracks, there's no Auto-Tune, there's nothing to hide, so why not allow it? Why wouldn't we want people to share their favorite moments of the show with their friends and family? People see stuff online and then want to seek it out for their own personal experience. Are there going to be wrong notes, missed choreography, and other imperfections? Yes. Every show. But that's what makes us what we are. Real. It's part of the charm.

SM: There is spontaneity and playfulness that we bring that is possible because of our friendships and that we have known each other for half of our lives. We can go off-script (that we write, no less) or try something that is unscripted each night, knowing that there are other people behind us who are listening, interacting, and working to make a "bit" the best it can be. For Chasers who come multiple times, I think they come as much, if not more, for the humor as the music.

As for offstage interaction, there is no magic bullet. You have to want to speak with people, be interested in what and who they are, and appreciate that in this world where there are millions of entertainment options, they have chosen to spend their night or weekend watching you perform.

TYLER TREPP: We're like brothers. If I said we all got along and everything was great all the time, I'd be lying. We do go through long tours, and of course there are times where people don't get along. But, like any relationship, we talk it out as a group or individually with another person and keep going. At the end of the day, it's all about this group and these 10 guys. That's the most important thing.

DN: We sing some serious and artful songs, and hopefully sing them well, but we punctuate those songs with jokes in our intros, or much less serious songs in the set. Because we've established ourselves as being "boy next door" types, our fans want us to be successful in more serious undertakings, just as you would want your nephew or best friend to sound good in the school talent show.

I interact with fans as much as I can via social media. I know hundreds of their names. I accept every friend request on Facebook and respond to direct messages personally. I do this because I feel like I owe it to them. We have at least four fans (that I could name off the top of my head) that have been to over 100 shows. Over 100. That's a lot. But I'd be lying if I said I wasn't aware of the positive impact this has on our business.

DS: I've heard many times that people like the SNC version of a given song more than the original. How do you approach an arrangement to make it your own and connect with the audience?

WC: As an arranger, it's easy to "cover" any song. What's difficult is making it impactful. Since we are on the road more than most groups, our arrangements need to be performance based first (studio tracks secondary). Our arrangements stay fluid to change as we see what sections of a song work or don't work on stage. If we can sell a song on stage, it will translate on an album, as our audience will seek it out.

As for fans liking our arrangements more than the original, I think that has to do with the stripped-down version they are hearing us do. Overproduction of some original tracks can turn a casual listener off. By simplifying it down to just vocals, the heart of the tracks is exposed.

TT: Arrangements can be approached a variety of ways, and every guy in the group does it differently. I'm a piano player, so I'm usually using a piano when I start my arrangements. Sometimes

THE HEART OF VOCAL HARMONY

I'll just have an idea and roll with it. Like what if we mashed up these two songs, they sound alike. Or what about this song done in this style? Other times it will take me a while to flesh it out. I also have a guy in the group who's kind of my buffer. I'll send him voice notes of me singing (terribly and forgetting half the words) or playing an idea to see what he thinks. If he likes it, I start to demo it; if not, I usually scrap it.

Connecting with the audience is tricky. Sometimes what you think will be good in the show as you're rehearsing it isn't. And sometimes a song you think wouldn't go over well, does. The good thing about performing live shows is that you can tell how a song is going to do almost immediately. So a lot of what we do is trial and error.

SI: Personally, my focus is to create original concepts, creative ideas, and humorous moments that will reach a wide audience. When I'm thinking about an arrangement or an idea, I put myself in the audience's seat. What will I be shocked by? What will make me think, "Wow, that was really clever," or, "I could never have imagined those two songs going together"? Coming from that place is risky, because not everything works, but it's a risk worth taking, because when you get one that hits, there's nothing like that moment of response from the audience.

SM: I believe our best results come when we put our own spin on a song. This could be through mashing up two songs, performing a song originally done by a female, or doing a song in a new style. Of course, this is much more difficult to do, takes much more time, and requires far more creativity, but the payoff is greater.

Once the arrangement is done, the soloist needs to find a way to honor the original without trying to replicate it. Many of the artists we cover are some of the greatest of all time. No one wants to see us do an impression; they want to see what we can bring to a song. So the first step is to find out how the song works in your voice and, if there is movement, in your body. Once you have those aspects down, the stage is a playground. The connection the audience desires most is with the true you, so the quicker you can get out of your head and start performing (for the pleasure of the audience *and* your compatriots on stage), the better the reaction from the viewer will be.

DS: What is it about the holidays that turns people toward vocal music, and how can those principles be carried throughout the year?

SI: When you think of Christmas music, what scene do you imagine? Carolers? Crowding around the piano in the living room with family singing favorite holiday songs? Church choirs? What's the common denominator here? Vocals. It's the best way to express emotion, and the holidays are a time of doing just that. There's a sense of community when listening to vocal music, which ties perfectly to the holidays.

WC: There is a purity to the holidays that lends itself to vocal music. Caroling is something that exists exclusively during the holidays. How we have used those principles and carried them throughout the year is by using the momentum of our holiday success to then allow us to be a non-holiday band. We don't shy away from performing "The Twelve Days of Christmas" in July. We don't try to act like our holiday albums and our winter tour are not the drivers for our entire year's success. We design our year around the holiday season, and by doing so, we are able to surprise our first-time audience members with our ability to be a successful year-round ensemble.

TT: For years people have associated vocal music with holiday music. Christmas carols are old. I think "Hark the Herald Angels Sing" was written in, like, the 1700s. So they've sung them in church for that long. A lot of choirs have sung Christmas carols, as well as the four carolers you see outside your town's Christmas tree lighting ceremony. So when you hear those songs you just associate them with voices, which is unlike any other genre of music.

SM: Holiday music is the one genre where a cappella and more "legit" singing never went out of style. The holidays are rooted in traditions, be they familial or societal, and in these forums, our type of music has always been in favor. For instance, think of how many children grew up singing the "Ukrainian Bell Carol" ("Carol of the Bells") in school choir. If it wasn't done a cappella, it was with a Spartan accompaniment that totally highlighted the vocals. Quite simply, vocal-centric holiday music has been kept alive and popular by schools, churches, communities, and families.

Also, while there are constant additions to the holiday catalog as new artists try their hand at classic tunes, the true classics remain. I grew up listening to Andy Williams, Barbra Streisand, Bing Crosby, Nat King Cole, and the list goes on and on. These aren't "flavor of the month" singers; these are classic artists of the past 70 years singing songs that have stood the test of time and tradition. And it is only with holiday music that this sense of tradition has continued to dominate a genre, hence our reverence for the more pure vocal sound this time of year.

JC: Vocal music is real as it gets. Live a cappella to me is the truest form of music. No drums, guitar, or producer to hide behind. It's raw and out there. The holidays are perfect for vocal music because of the messages of praise and uplifting people. The purity of hearing the human voice while shopping, decorating, relaxing with family is tradition. I'm more than delighted to be part of that tradition.

SINGERS

Everyone loves to sing, but it takes a special something to be a great vocal harmony singer. You need to give as much as you take, you need to listen twice as hard to weave your voice in and out of others', you need to be prepared for the many ways the unique sound of other voices can change from night to night.

Jerry Lawson

Before everything that exists now in vocal music, there were the Persuasions: the original genre-bending pioneers who blended old and new to create a sound that for over 40 years brought audiences to their feet and inspired generations of singers. Out front was a soulful powerhouse of a lead singer who deserves many more accolades than he has received: Jerry Lawson.

DEKE SHARON: You almost singlehandedly kept popular a cappella going in the 1970s. What was the reaction from audiences then, and has it changed over time?

JERRY LAWSON: The reaction was unbelievable. I was astonished to see how people were so excited. They were on their feet applauding, always wanting more; it seemed like they could never get enough. I wouldn't say it changed over time. There are still people who have never seen or heard anything like what we do.

DS: You've performed a cappella for over 40 years with the Persuasions and Talk of the Town, and also performed with instruments. As a lead singer, how do the two differ?

JL: Without instruments it's so much harder. There is hardly room to rest your voice or make mistakes, which can easily be covered by a band. With a band a vocalist gets lots of rest, and with a band a vocalist doesn't sweat so much.

DS: Perhaps no one alive has been more involved with a cappella for longer than you. What lessons from the past should young singers know?

JL: They need to be dedicated, practice hard, stay on their notes, be professional, arrive on time for rehearsals, and never turn their back to the audience. I would hope they would care enough to study the history and listen to the masters who came before them, such as the Mills Brothers, the Harmonizing Four, the Four Aces, Sam Cooke and the Soul Stirrers, the Five Blind Boys of Mississippi, the Blind Boys of Alabama, the Oakridge Boys, the Gaither Singers, the Golden Gate Quartet, the Persuasions, and Sweet Honey in the Rock. Bernice Johnson Reagan was amazing!

DS: My favorite judges' comment on *The Sing-Off* came from Ben Folds in Season One: "It wasn't perfect, but I didn't care!" What would you say to critics who emphasize precision over passion?

JL: What can I say? I agree. If you can carry the tune with passion and touch the souls of others, it shouldn't have to be perfect.

Blake Lewis

Many members of the a cappella community have done well on *American Idol*, but none better than Blake, who was the runner-up in the show's sixth season. Prior to that he was a member of Seattle's cutting-edge pop a cappella band Kickshaw. Now he blends pop, hip-hop, and electronica in his solo/beatbox/live looping shows around the world.

DEKE SHARON: How did your early experiences in a cappella help make you a better soloist and performer?
BLAKE LEWIS: Kickshaw was a crash course on vocal blend and performance as well as the business side at every show. I also really honed my craft as a beatboxer and vocal percussionist in this group. As a performer and soloist, there was a lot of freedom in our group because every show we always improvised and made up a song for the audience. With all our vocal effects we used, I took it to the next level, incorporating loop pedals, Kaoss pads, and many other fx. You gotta remember this was in 1999, before anyone was really doing that, so I made my presence known in Seattle. People were always saying, "Hey, did you check out that dude with the crazy lit-up pedal board?!" I was so into it. Strobe lights and LEDs all glowed in my plexiglass case. I just wanted to be remembered.

DS: You were known for your beatboxing on *American Idol* as well as your solo singing. How does each technique inform the other?
BL: They are one and the same to me. I started beatboxing and vocal scratching because I do voice-overs for cartoons and beatboxing came in to my life subconsciously until I saw Matthew Selby (formerly of m-pact). That day was the game changer. You couldn't shut me up. I was constantly beatboxing. It wasn't until I got into Kickshaw that I was inclined to balance it and really listen to my voice. My style of beatboxing is very vocal. I try and keep the beats simple now, to allow my singing to sit nicely on top of it when I record a loop at a show or in the studio when I'm creating. I've really worked on my balance as a vocalist and a beatboxer. The greatest thing about beatboxing is that it's instant groove. The voice is the most powerful and creative instrument ever.

DS: Nobody gets to the finals of *American Idol* without captivating audiences and touching hearts. What do you do to maximize the emotional power of your performances?

BL: I really try and convey the lyrics in my performances. I've been in a couple musicals where you have to learn to project in character. When I'm on stage, I transform into what I think is the best version of myself. I'm more comfortable and I'm way more connected than I am in any other environment. *American Idol* gave me the best stage to try and connect with as many people as I could fathom. It was so surreal and so much fun.

DS: Now you tour as a solo artist, using live looping equipment to display your a cappella, beatbox, and solo skills simultaneously. How do you keep songs raw and emotional and honest while interfacing so much with technology?

BL: Keep it simple. When looping, I put my drums on one channel, bass and harmonies on others. I really love building something new in front of an audience. I usually take suggestions or bring people on stage so I can sample them. With my sampler, I just record whatever comes to me at the time. Lots of vocal stutters and fun reverb/delay throws, and whatever else the song needs. Really fun!

DS: It's just you on stage, no one to hide behind or give you a break. Do you have any techniques to prepare yourself before jumping on stage? How do you stay focused and engaged through the entire performance?

BL: This is funny to me, cause I'm super ADD on stage. I'm full of energy and the only way I stay focused and engaged is if I rehearse and write a very thought-out set list in advance. If not, I lose my mind and lose focus. Also, I warm up 30 minutes prior to hitting the stage, but that's about it.

Christòpheren Nomura

All of us have someone we idolized while growing up, someone impossibly cool a few years older who acted as both role model and inspiration. For me, that person was Chris Nomura. Without him, I would never have heard of or joined the Tufts Beelzebubs, and my life would be immeasurably different. His career took him into professional classical solo singing, opera, and most recently a lead role in George Takei's Broadway musical *Allegiance*, in which he plays the stern, traditional father figure, punctuating each line with his resonant baritone.

DEKE SHARON: Like me, you were a member of the San Francisco Boys Chorus, Town School Choir, and University High School Camerata. How did your early experiences singing in choirs prepare you for life as a professional singer?

CHRISTÒPHEREN NOMURA: My early experiences, especially with the San Francisco Boys Chorus, serve as the foundation for my work today. Reading music, ear training, vocal technique, and the discipline to continuously practice were always emphasized and stressed since I was four years old. The thing is, I loved it. It was never "work" for me and I could never understand why others would hate it.

DS: At Tufts you were a member of the Beelzebubs. What lessons did you learn from male collegiate a cappella?

CN: My time in collegiate a cappella was about simply having fun and making music with a bunch of guys who liked to sing and perform as much as I did. It also brought me back to my Boys Chorus roots, since I was singing with guys again. I was comfortable. I was with my brothers. We worked hard for a common goal—and had a blast doing it at the same time. The difference now was that we were becoming men—so we were sharing real life experiences along with our music at the same time. The bonding times were powerful because we hardly ever had an "off" season. It was a constant throughout the year.

DS: Most of your life you have performed classical music. How is emotion generally approached and discussed within the world of classical soloists?

CN: Well, emotion has to come from within you as an artist, and it is essential in everything you do. Yes, you have to learn the words, the notes, the phrasing, but what brings that song, aria, or role to life? It should be your choices. They can and should change and evolve the more times you study and perform a piece. Performing in front of audiences helps you make those discoveries. You can practice forever, but until you feel the sensations within you in a concert setting, you will never really know the true emotion that a piece or role holds for you.

DS: You have sung popular music, opera, and art songs, and now have a lead role on Broadway—all very different musical and performing styles. What are the similarities and differences in the way you express emotion in each?

CN: Having a lead role on Broadway is very similar to a lead role in opera or even art song in terms of expressing emotion. Whether you are singing in Italian, Russian, German, or English should make no difference, right? Well, for me, there is a difference. Since English is my native tongue and I express myself primarily in this language, I am much more comfortable and flexible singing my American Broadway role. Also, singing a Broadway role is extremely beneficial for growth and discovery since you are performing it every day and sometimes twice a day, versus an opera production with perhaps three performances in total or three shows per week for a two- or three-week run. With *Allegiance*, we just finished our 160th show over the last four months. The range of emotion can be pretty wide, depending on where you want to go with it that day or night or how you are feeling—certainly something that every actor can explore more easily when doing it daily. For that reason, I love the everyday experience of the Broadway show.

DS: Your role in *Allegiance* is an emotionally charged one. How did you prepare for it? What experiences do you draw upon, both your own and others'?

CN: I drew my role directly from my father. It was easier than I thought. As an American-born performer, I thought it would be a much bigger challenge to use the correct dialect, body language, posture, facial expressions, and gestures, just to name a few. But in the end, playing the role of a Japanese father during World War II was both fulfilling and rewarding. I learned so much about myself, my dad (who passed away 15 years ago), and the Japanese culture which I am unfortunately far away from, living in the suburbs of New Jersey. There is no question that this experience has brought me closer to my roots and understanding of what my parents endured moving to this country as immigrants.

Samantha Waldman

More than any other member, Samantha Waldman represented
the heart of Stay Tuned during the year they appeared on Lifetime
Television's *Pitch Slapped*. Not glamorous, yet charismatic. Not a
technical superstar in any specific musical category, yet harboring
a deep honesty that is more compelling than flash when polished
and given an opportunity to shine. Sam's journey was the group's
journey, which is why she continued to find herself in the lime-
light. I decided to reach out to ask Sam her impressions of our time
together because I was curious what it was like for her on the other
side of the camera.

DEKE SHARON: Why did you first join choir? Why do you sing? Why
did you join Stay Tuned?
SAMANTHA WALDMAN: Choir was always a part of the high school
equation for me. D-Wing (the wing all of the music groups are
located in) was in my blood. I called myself a D-winger before I had
even set foot in high school. I joined choir because when I sing
and make harmony with other people I feel like I can truly define
happiness at its purest. The warmth that spreads through me when
I sing is irreplaceable. I sing not because I like to or because I want
to, but because in order for me to genuinely feel and connect with
other people, I need to.

Stay Tuned was the coolest thing in my eyes. When they were
created, they were the local equivalent of Pentatonix for me, albeit
four times bigger. While I appreciate the beauty of choral pieces,
contemporary pop music always had my heart. I knew that if I
performed pop music, I'd be able to put just a sliver more of myself
into the music. The group was kooky and full of raw talent, but before you, we definitely lacked the work ethic and emotional drive it
took to put together quality a cappella performances.

DS: What were your first impressions of our process working together?
SW: I don't think I've ever liked anyone more in the first five
seconds of knowing someone. You reminded me of, well, me in the
way you were such a music nerd and you didn't care who knew it. I
loved your process, because as much of a stickler as I am about the
technical aspects of music, I knew that we didn't focus enough on
the message behind our songs. Also, my first impression of a cappella music was the idea of emulating the instruments our voices

replaced, and before you I had been disappointed to see that most a cappella arrangements don't do that.

DS: What was it like having everything captured on camera? Did it make things easier or more difficult? What was different about rehearsals during the filming?

SW: Having a camera there to capture our every move made things more complicated. Music and the process that goes into making good, genuine music is raw and emotional and uncensored, but knowing that anything I said or did could end up on national television made me restrict myself more than I normally would have. I definitely held back because of it.

Rehearsals with you were more productive than ever before in my experience with Stay Tuned. Your work ethic and need to create something amazing were both contagious. The way you approached us as equals in the musical journey encouraged us to be all in with what we did. We had our moments where we needed to be reeled in, but you taught us how and where to draw the line between hard work and enjoying the ride.

DS: How did the group change and grow over eight weeks? What were the best moments?

SW: Over the eight weeks we had with you, Stay Tuned grew into something entirely different. Where before our end goal was winning, we learned that winning should be an afterthought. I was one of the worst offenders of that. If you're only singing to win a shiny piece of metal, why do it? Shouldn't it be for an entirely different reason? Not to mention how much better we expressed emotion! We let go of the notes for once and actually put meaning into the songs. I personally found that the tuning was better when we focused on the meaning, the "why" of it all. We were completely different after just eight weeks with you, and I still can't believe it.

Some of our best moments came from bouncing ideas off of each other. We all had such completely different styles, and in the moments we managed to work together we came up with the best overall products. Our deepest, most connected moments together are the ones that stand out most vividly in my mind.

DS: When did we stumble? How did we recover?

SW: A group of 21 loud, opinionated people doesn't always mesh perfectly. Our biggest obstacles came from a lack of respect for each other's ideas and feelings. The tension that was sometimes a result of that often impacted how we performed and vibed off of each other. The only way to recover from something like that is to take a step back and remember the big picture. Stay Tuned is a huge dysfunctional family, but a family nonetheless. Once we reminded ourselves of that, we found that we could do anything.

DS: What do you think of everything now, looking back? How have you changed as a result of our time together?

SW: Looking back, all I could ask for is more time. This was the best experience of my life to date, and sometimes I still can't believe it happened. In retrospect, I really wouldn't change a thing. Sure, being on camera was weird and uncomfortable at times, but it gave us a chance to sit down and think about what a cappella really is when you boil it down to the basics. I don't think any true a cappella geek can actually put into words what this music really is, but we came pretty close to doing that this summer.

I feel like a completely different person after spending so much time with you. I take the time to appreciate the beauty around me, be it through music or anything else. I think about how everything I do impacts other people, and I act less and less for myself and more and more for the people I love. And, while it's still a huge part of me, I find myself ignoring the music snob in me, and I've officially taken up the mantra "Anyone can sing."

DS: What have you learned that others should know?

SW: Above all else, sing because it makes you happy. Don't do it for a resume-filler, to please your friends, parents, or anyone else. Do it because it makes you feel warm from head to toe and because it allows you to make connections with other people that you wouldn't have been able to otherwise.

Conclusion

A work of art which did not begin in emotion is not art.
—PAUL CEZANNE

Powerful unified emotional singing isn't easy, but vocal harmony itself is rarely easy. You spend hours if not days perfecting a single song, so you know what it means to spend time creating something great. The good news is that once you have invested time creating consistently heartfelt performances, it gets easier. The unification of emotion will erase many of the problems you have been addressing in rehearsal, including vowel matching, phrasing, dynamics, and the like. Your group will sing together in a more unified way because they will be more unified.

When beginning this book, I made it clear there was no simple list, no easy way to deliver every emotion with just a few words or commands, but now that you understand the many principles within these pages and have completed the process in your mind, I will give you a list, a ten-step process that you can now approach with a deeper understanding of what these seemingly simple steps entail:

1. Know the **concepts** central to great vocal harmony singing.
2. **Prepare** yourself, your group, your environment.
3. Understand the **emotions** and messages you can best present.
4. **Choose** a song and how you will perform it.
5. Determine your own **meaning** knowing the song's lyric, history, and context.
6. Help your singers find their own personal **perspective**.
7. Bring together musical and emotional **technique**.
8. Refine the song, **considering** what your singers need at each juncture.
9. Provide **motivation** before and during performance.
10. Look for **insights** from all sources in perpetuity.

You'll notice that each of the bold words reflects a section of this book. In essence, everything you've read in these pages up to the interviews has been a single list, a process that takes time to understand but ultimately results in 10 steps you can use each time you approach a new song. Refer back to any of the chapters as necessary, write notes in the margins, and share this book with your singers, so they too can understand that emotional singing is within their reach.

And there it is. Your journey doesn't end here; rather, you find yourself on the same path that brought you to this book: the desire for more knowledge, better practices, better understanding how to make great music and transform the lives of your singers and audience. The way to do that remains the same as it always has been: make lots of music. Trial and error is the only way to learn what really works for you and for your audience. As they say on shampoo bottles, "Lather, rinse, repeat." Great emotional singing isn't a destination, it's a journey, one to be taken time and again to different places with different moods and different audiences. There is a great deal of imprecision in almost any human endeavor, especially something as ephemeral as music, so it will take time, practice, patience, and analysis to learn how to make a reliably powerful musical and emotional experience for you, your singers, and your audience.

And then, once you do, you're going to want to do it all over again.

Acknowledgments

I read upwards of 70 books a year, and yet I don't think I look at the acknowledgments more than once a decade. Nonetheless, I forge onward in hopes that you are a more thorough reader than I, as the following people deserve much credit and respect for the selfless help they provided me through the process of writing this book.

Tom Carter, whose *Choral Charisma* is a fantastic book on the marriage of choral singing and method acting, provided much inspiration throughout these pages.

All of the esteemed musicians who gave their time to answer my questions: there is a place in heaven for you all, instruments optional.

The fine musical minds who proofread my early drafts, offering your edits and advice: like the church that has every brick and beam replaced over time yet calls itself the original church, I shall claim ownership of every word and thought in these pages, even if they all came from you. Aca-luminaries Meg Alexander, Kari Francis, Elie Landau, and Amy Malkoff, alongside J.D. Frizzell, Brody McDonald, Tom Paster, John DeFerraro, and Ben Spalding, all exemplary directors, all served as my vanguards, slogging through my first draft. For that they should be canonized.

And, finally, my lovely nuclear family, Katy, Cap, and Mimi Sharon, all of whom helped me refine my thoughts and provided endless support through the fall of 2015, when I said no to everything else and yes to being a husband and dad: driving my daughter to school, getting the house repainted and reroofed, putting away the seemingly endless urban flotsam and jetsam that appears throughout our house at all hours, cooking dinner each night, and writing this book. Oh, and many adventure dessert nights, during which time we sampled the seemingly endless offerings around San Francisco. Please recommend this book to a friend to help pay our dental bills.

ACKNOWLEDGMENTS

Thanks also to the keen eyes who carefully picked through my final draft: Stefanie Chase, Kathryn Webster, Anne Marie Fowler, Kimberly Nguyen, Sam Dantowitz, Katherine Girvin, Lulu Picart, Rich Payton, and my very first choral director at age five: Michael Secour.